921
PAINE   Meltzer, Milton

Tom Paine

DUE DATE   **BRODART   05/97   25.80**

❖ TOM PAINE ❖
VOICE OF REVOLUTION

By Milton Meltzer

FRANKLIN WATTS
A Division of Grolier Publishing

❖ New York ❖ London ❖ Hong Kong ❖ Sydney ❖
Danbury, Connecticut

Photographs ©: American Philosophical Society: pp. 122, 137, 148, 152, 162; The Bettmann Archive: pp. 8, 21, 27, 31, 36, 40, 54, 58, 75, 83, 90, 92, 108, 117, 126, 133, 140, 146; Colonial Williamsburg: p. 29; Corbis-Bettmann: pp. 13, 16, 46, 79, 114; Courtesy of the Thetford Library: p. 165; The Library Company of Philadelphia: p. 19; The Library of Congress: p. 66; The Metropolitan Museum of Art: p. 49; The New York Public Library Picture Collection: p. 42, 53; The New York Public Library Prints Division: p. 35; The New-York Historical Society: p. 99; UPI/Bettmann: p. 160.

Library of Congress Cataloging-in-Publication Data
Meltzer, Milton, 1915–
      Tom Paine : voice of revolution / by Milton Meltzer
          p.   cm.
      Includes bibliographical references and index.
      Summary: The story of the self-educated craftsman who earned a place in history as the voice of the American Revolution.
      ISBN 0-531-11291-8
      1. Paine, Thomas, 1737–1809—Juvenile literature. 2. Political scientists—United States—Biography—Juvenile literature.
      3. Revolutionaries—United States—Biography—Juvenile Literature.
      [1. Paine, Thomas, 1737—1809. 2. Political scientists.
      3. Revolutionaries.] I. Title.
      JC178.V2M45 1996
      320.5'1'092—dc20
      [B]   96–11956
                                              CIP
                                            AC

All rights reserved. Published simultaneously in Canada.
Printed in the United States of America.

1 2 3 4 5 6 7 8 9 10 R 05 04 03 02 01 00 99 98 97 96

❖ CONTENTS ❖

THOMAS PAINE.

❖ FOREWORD ❖

Say Tom Paine's name and how do people respond?

First, to most, it's only faintly recognizable.

Oh yes, some will say—the American Revolution! Didn't he have something to do with it?

So he did, but what?

He wrote one of the most remarkable political pamphlets in all history. *Common Sense*, it was called. It was published January 10, 1776, six months before the Continental Congress approved the Declaration of Independence. It had an enormous success, for it helped bring about the Revolution by making Americans realize that independence from Britain was their true goal and that republican government was vastly superior to hereditary monarchy.

Paine's pamphlet sold in the hundreds of thousands, making it the first best-seller in American history. It had a powerful effect on the decision to fight for independence from Britain. It was lucky for America that Paine proved to be the right man in the right place at the right time.

Who was this man? He was important, notably in that crucial revolutionary year of 1776. Not long after, going abroad, he became a vital force in the French Revolution of 1789. And his ideas did much to spark the growing movement for democracy and equality in his home country of England. Worldwide, his ideas are still an inspiration and a guide to peoples everywhere seeking to make a better and freer life for themselves and their communities.

Radical thinkers and activists never have an easy time of it. Paine, as one historian writes, was "Both deeply admired and deeply despised." Although he sometimes enjoyed honors, he often suffered insults. With his difficult personality, he could both win friends and make enemies. He never knew prosperity and died penniless and alone.

This is the story of a self-educated craftsman who earned a place in history as the voice of the American Revolution. He once said, "Above all, I defend the cause of humanity. My country is the world, and my religion is to do good."

❖ 1 ❖

APPRENTICE AND PRIVATEER

If one word can characterize the first half of Tom Paine's life that word is failure. Just about everything he tried to do in these early decades didn't work out. No one could have predicted he would prove himself to be one of the world's great original thinkers.

His life began in Thetford, a small town in Norfolk County, England. The year was 1737, the day, Saturday, January 29. The infant's parents were Joseph Paine and Frances Cocke. They came from widely separated classes. Tom's mother was the daughter of a socially prominent lawyer. Hers was an Anglican family, members of the Church of England. Tom's father, by contrast, was the son of a shoemaker who had to supplement a small income with tenant farming. As a boy, Joseph Paine was apprenticed to a corset maker, a poorly paid trade that he would practice all his life. He was raised as a Quaker, but when he married Frances Cocke, the Anglican, the Quakers expelled him from their community.

The infant was baptized an Anglican and later, around the age of twelve, was confirmed by the Anglican bishop. So the boy was raised in a mixed-religion family, in a community where Anglicanism and Quakerism were at odds. The Quakers were a devoutly religious society that saw toleration as a serious heresy. When your immortal soul was at stake, to tolerate another faith in this world was to pay for it in the next.

The Quakers were nonconformists who dissented from the doctrine of the Church of England. English law permitted a degree of toleration for faiths other than the official Anglican church, but still, Quakers suffered many kinds of discrimination in everyday life. They were denied the right to vote or to hold public office, and they could not enter the public universities at Oxford or Cambridge.

Quakers like Tom's father mistrusted religious and governmental authority. The son acquired that suspicion of authority. So too did the young Tom absorb the Quaker belief in inner spiritual light of the divine that inspired Quakers to do good. But he also learned the Anglican catechism and studied the Bible so diligently that for the rest of his life he could recite long passages from memory.

From parents who practiced different faiths, Tom learned how a family could live together peacefully if they agreed to disagree about religion while cooperating with one another on all else. In the end, Quaker beliefs—including pacifism, the opposition to war and violence—had the greater influence on Paine's life and work.

Four churches served Thetford's two thousand people. The Quakers were the only nonconformists, and their meeting house was small, holding just fifty people. It was located next to Thetford's jail. The thatched cottage of Tom's family was close to Gallows Hill, where convicted criminals were brought for hanging. The jail, three stories high, was a stony symbol of England's cruel punishment system. During the nineteen years young Tom spent in Thetford, he saw men and women from all over the country herded into the dark and filthy prison to await trial and sentencing.

He could easily identify with the ragged, shambling figures, fearful of their fate. An apprentice who robbed his master of a trifling sum was ordered to be transported to the American colonies. A dishonest trader was sent to the ducking stool on the river Thet. Others were sentenced to be branded, or put in the pillory, or whipped publicly, or fined, or imprisoned. Many of the offenses were crimes against property, committed out of poverty and hunger.

Death sentences were handed down casually by the Lord Chief Justice. You could go to the gallows for stealing twenty shillings, for stealing a bushel of wheat from a barn, for stealing a parcel of tea. After sentencing, the convicted ones were chained to the prison floor overnight, and at eight the next morning they were walked past the Paine cottage and up Gallows Hill. There, before a gaping crowd, they were swung into oblivion.

Few prisoners were executed for murder. But under a vicious penal system all sorts of petty offenses earned capital punishment. A servant who stole from his master or a farm laborer who stole a sheep ended life on the gallows. But if you were rich and killed someone, you were acquitted or got off with a mild sentence. There was, Tom gradually realized, one law for the rich and another law for the poor. In his time at least two hundred capital offenses blackened the books. And most of them were designed to protect the absolute rights of private property.

Executions in eighteenth century England, by hanging or beheading, were made a public spectacle.

Tom was seven when his parents sent him to Thetford Grammar School. It was just a five-minute walk from home. The school was hundreds of years old, and in Tom's time had about thirty boy pupils. In earlier days it had confined itself to educating "gentlemen's sons" on a steady diet of classical Greek and Latin. The Quakers rejected the notion that training in Greek and Roman rhetoric and history was the best preparation for life. Under the increasing pressure of tradespeople like the Paines the school began to offer such modern studies as arithmetic, accounting, French, and science. Although the school fee was quite small, Tom's parents had trouble paying it.

Tom did well in science and mathematics and enjoyed reading such "poetical" authors as William Shakespeare, John Milton, and John Bunyan, some of whose books were in the small school library. He began trying his hand at poetry, as witness the few surviving lines of his attempts at age eight:

> *Here lies the body of John Crow,*
> *Who once was high but now is low;*
> *Ye brother Crows take warning all,*
> *For as you rise, so must you fall.*

The poem was inspired by the loss of a pet crow that he buried in his backyard.

On his father's insistence, Tom took no course in Latin, for Mr. Paine believed drilling youngsters in those languages only trained them to be obedient to the authority of those in power.

Tom's schooling ended after five years. At twelve he was taken out of school to serve a standard seven-year apprenticeship to his father. The craft of making corsets was demanding. Women of the better-off classes wore corsets stiffened with whalebone and laced at the back. The young apprentice tried to be patient during his long hours of cutting and shaping woolen cloth, boning between each row of stitching, and lining the patterned stay with linen.

But he could never like the work. He was too restless to stick with work that called for such steady effort.

Such an apprenticeship might have led to a partnership with his father, but business dropped off badly by the time his seven years were almost up. There never were enough upper-class women locally to provide a sizable market, and competitive corset makers from London and other regional towns sent salesmen into Thetford to further cut Mr. Paine's business. The town had been suffering hard times as outside traders came into the local market. One traveler, passing through Thetford, described the town as "very poor and mean, much decayed of late years, many houses dropping down not worth repairing."

Tom was eager for a more exciting life than his father's. At school, he had relished a teacher's tales of adventures on a man-of-war, roving the high seas to India, Africa, the West Indies, and North America. The schoolmaster loaned Tom a history of the Virginia colony, which made the boy dream of a marvelous life in that strange and distant world. It's likely too that he read such travel books as Daniel Defoe's *Robinson Crusoe* (1720) and Jonathan Swift's *Gulliver's Travels* (1726).

One day in the fall of 1756 Tom noticed a newspaper advertisement for men who wished to try their fortune and "as well to serve their King and Country" by signing on to a privateer cruising against the French. The ship, named the *Terrible*, was captained by William Death.

This was the time of the Seven Years' War (known as the French and Indian Wars in the American colonies). The English and French empires had been competing for world supremacy for more than fifty years. The fighting had just spilled over into America, as the two powers, with large holdings on the continent, contended for control of the Ohio Valley.

The crews of most privateers sailed not for glory or patriotism but for profit. It was a kind a piracy, for though these ships were privately owned, they were licensed by the British government to attack enemy merchant ships

In 1757 Paine sailed on a privateer much like this one lying offshore awaiting its crew.

and seize their cargo. The booty was split among the captain, the officers, and the crew. Tom signed on, but before he could go abroad, his father learned of the project and begged him not to go. It was lucky that he stayed on shore. For Tom soon read in the newspapers that the *Terrible* had fought a losing battle with a French privateer. About 150 crewmen of the *Terrible* died, including the captain and all but one of the officers.

What to do now? He had to find work. It happened quickly, because of a strike organized by journeymen corset makers who demanded a shorter work day. They were among the first craftsmen in England to organize a trade union. London masters operated on a 6:00 A.M. to 8:00 P.M. schedule. The union wanted those fourteen hours cut by one. Tom took a job even though it meant scabbing on the strikers. Apparently at this time in his life Paine had no sympathy for the union. The job he found paid a modest wage, just enough to buy food and rent a shabby little room in the Covent Garden district.

The long working hours and rigid control by a master grated on Tom. This wasn't much better than being a slave on an American plantation. In January 1757 he quit the job to sign on to another privateer that needed men. The two-hundred foot *King of Prussia*, with two heavily armed gun decks, left port with 250 men on board. The majority were needed not to handle the vessel but to do the fighting.

And Tom expected to share in the fighting for he knew how violent privateering would be. Yet he set aside the pacifist principles of his Quaker upbringing. Was it out of patriotic duty to his country at war? Or the prospect of profits? Or maybe to savor the thrill of defying his father's authority?

He found that life aboard ship was harsh: long stretches of boring routine, cold and damp night watch, bad food, rats and roaches everywhere. If you didn't die in a battle at sea, then disease might kill you. Tom saw plenty of action half a dozen times when enemy ships were seized and their cargoes taken. At the end of six months the *King of Prussia* docked at the port of Dartmouth, its marauding days over. Tom's share of the loot was thirty pounds, a large sum for a man used to just getting by. He never tried going to sea again. His luck held this time, but maybe it wouldn't next time. Besides, unknown adventures lay ahead in the great city of London.

❖ 2 ❖

LIFE IN LONDON

At twenty, Tom was slim and athletic, about five feet ten, with intense blue eyes "full of fire," "the eyes of an apostle," someone who knew him said. His thick dark-brown hair he wore pulled back into a ponytail. Friends from his London days reported he was soft-spoken, with a Norfolk accent, serious, intelligent, eager to learn. And he had money in his pocket!

London at that time had a population of about half a million. In all England there were only some six million people. Cities like Manchester, Liverpool, or Birmingham were small by modern measure, all of them with populations under fifty thousand. Travelers' accounts show London was a squalid city, lacking in common conveniences. The streets were unpaved and narrow, and with no sanitary system they stank. The houses of the poor were one- or two-room hovels and desperately overcrowded. Ten to a room was not uncommon. Often the rooms had no furniture, not even beds. Disease was rampant, and death a routine event. Infant mortality was high. With death so all-threatening, people sought any means to ease the pain: drink, gambling, violence. The police force was far too small to curb the burning, looting, and destruction of mob actions. Yet people from the country kept migrating into the towns in an endless stream.

Paine spent the autumn and winter months of 1757–58 in the Covent Garden district. With his share of the privateer's profits, he could put off seeking work and take in what London had to offer.

The contrast between the luxury of the rich and the

The lives of London's poor observed by Paine are depicted in William Hogarth's contemporary print Gin Lane.

poverty of the masses was glaring. The craftsmen and artisans, like Paine, were a class between the rich and the poor. They worked long hours for modest wages that kept them above subsistence, but only so long as trade was good. When it went down, as it often and unpredictably did, hunger and poverty filled life with anxiety.

As industry began to change, with the introduction of labor-saving machinery, the craftsmen felt all the more threatened. When they joined forces to insist on their rights to a decent living, Parliament passed laws against forming unions. Still, journeymen kept getting together in their friendly societies and in the taverns. Many of them were literate, and the few newspapers that spoke for them helped focus their sense of grievance and injustice.

Far greater in number than the craftsmen and journeymen were the mass of London's population. These were the laborers, who had only their muscle and sweat to offer. They never enjoyed steady jobs and depended on casual work. They could be dismissed at will, plunging at once into abject poverty.

To the politicians, the mass of Londoners were a nightmare. Desperately poor, they could easily be summoned to riot in the streets. The poor and propertyless had no political rights. Nor did anyone yet believe that they should have them. Tom had learned in Thetford how savage were the laws dealing with crimes against property. Here in London, he could see a child hanged from the gallows because he had swiped a handkerchief worth one shilling.

London's many bookshops were a great attraction for so curious a mind. Tom browsed their shelves, especially in search of books about science. "The natural bent of my mind was to science," he once said. He began to attend lectures by Benjamin Martin and James Ferguson, two men who traveled about England bringing the news of scientific discoveries to eager audiences denied advanced education. Martin was a mathematician and editor of a monthly magazine on science. He also made globes, two of which Tom bought.

Ferguson was a Scottish astronomer, a friend of Benjamin Franklin's who lived close by. Ferguson's book, *Astronomy Explained upon Sir Isaac Newton's Principles, and Made Easy to Those Who Have Not Studied Mathematics*, was happily received by readers like Paine eager to understand Newtonian ideas. Tom paid for a one-month course with Ferguson on the art of using globes, and then for another six months he sat in on public lectures given by both men on several aspects of science.

In the lecture halls Tom found new friends. The men and women who came were mostly self-educated artisans and shopkeepers. Many of them were dissenters from religious orthodoxy, with a bent toward political radicalism. They often heard the lecturers cite the words of the Elizabethan scientist Francis Bacon: "Knowledge is

*The astronomer James Ferguson, whose London lectures
Paine attended.*

power." Although the lecturers said little about politics, it was evident that such thinkers believed the expansion of knowledge about the real world should be developed by common effort and for the common good.

Newtonian thinkers held that there is a natural order of the material world, planned by God for the guidance and benefit of humanity. The same human reason that could discover the laws of nature could be applied to evaluating the way any political system functioned. If natural laws made the world beautiful and harmonious, sure-ly a science of government could be developed and applied to human institutions so that people could work and live together in happiness and freedom.

That line of thought made Tom question an established system that followed precedent rather than logic. So science and politics became connected in his mind. He felt there were vast regions of knowledge yet to be mapped, and why couldn't he be one of the explorers?

The wealthy and the powerful who governed England didn't like this trend of thought. The critical spirit of science applied to the existing institutions of government and property threatened trouble. A new political consciousness awakened in artisans like Tom Paine could breed movements for democracy and equality that England had never known.

❖ 3 ❖

PLAIN TALK

hen Tom's pockets emptied, he had to find work.
His savings ran out as the winter of 1757–58
ended. In April 1759 he left London for the port
town of Dover. There he found temporary work as a journeyman corset maker with a man named Benjamin Grace.
Hoping to establish a shop of his own, at the end of a year
he borrowed some money from Grace and moved to the
small town of Sandwich, southeast of London. In a cottage
on New Street he began business as a master corset maker.

Although the records are skimpy for this period, Paine
seems to have found time to do some preaching in the
Methodist chapel. Methodism had been founded by John
Wesley after a great mystical experience, around the time
that Paine was born. Forced out of the Anglican church as
a dissenter, Wesley took to the road, preaching wherever he
found an audience. He organized hundreds of Methodist
chapels, providing a spiritual home mainly for the poor.
Even though the poor were victims of inequality and injustice, Wesley was completely conservative in politics. He
detested radical thinkers. He believed the proper way to
get rid of the evils of society was to transform the individual. Salvation would come from doing good works; the
Methodist ideal was to lead people into an active, selfless
Christian life.

What seems to have drawn Paine to Methodism was
the way it brought together lonely and insecure people
(like himself?), especially the poor, to share in intimate
social relationships. Within each local chapel people often
learned to read and write, to speak up in public, to govern

themselves. Methodism nurtured self-respect and self-reliance. With a new sense of solidarity poor people could expand their horizons, moving beyond the borders of the established church and state.

Tom responded to preaching that held that Christ's sacrifice and atonement meant that everyone might be saved, not just the preordained elect. God's grace shone equally upon the rich and the poor. This opened up a vision of a free and equal community of souls making a life together on this earth.

As he preached, Paine for the first time was reaching out to other people, learning how to express himself in a way that touched hearts and minds. His "hearers," as they were called, were deaf to the stiff and boring sermons of Anglican preachers. Plain talk was what they responded to, down-to-earth language that echoed their own voices.

Speaking to their fears and worries, their dreams and desires, Tom came to recognize the potential power of these people as a social force. He did not hold with the Wesleyans of his time who believed in loyalty to the established order and the king. No, he was convinced that injustice did not have to be suffered eternally; it could be remedied. If only commoners would engage in public life and speak up for what they wanted, then change would be possible.

In 1759 Paine met Mary Lambert, "a pretty girl of modest behavior." She worked as a maid in the home of a wealthy merchant of Sandwich. After a summer's courtship they married. Almost nothing is known of Mary or the marriage. Soon after the young couple moved into a house, Tom's business dropped off badly, and Mary began a troubled pregnancy. Nothing seemed to go well. Perhaps for Mary's health, they moved ten miles (sixteen kilometers) to Margate, a fishing town known for its fresh sea air. When Mary went into labor, she was cared for by an experienced midwife, the common practice at the time. But she and her child died in delivery.

Now, after less than a year of marriage, Paine was alone. He smothered his grief, believing, as most men did, it was not manly to show emotion. Did that early tragic loss of wife and child numb his feelings permanently? He never talked about it. He would marry again, and divorce, but he had few close friends among women. In his writing he had little say about women, even about his mother, who lived a long life.

Unable to make a success of his trade, Tom had to find other ways to survive. What about becoming an exciseman? He had heard about that job from his wife, whose late father had done that work. Tom wrote to his father, asking what he thought. Mr. Paine replied at once, urging him to go ahead. So in the spring of 1761 Tom went to live with his parents in Thetford, while preparing for the entrance examination all candidates had to take.

Excisemen worked for the civil service. The job was to collect an internal customs duty, or tax, mostly on beer and ale, but also on such goods as tea, coffee, tobacco, chocolate, salt, and soap. It was not a great job. The pay was poor, and it meant spending long hours on the road, collecting the taxes and filing written reports with London headquarters. Tom would learn how disorganized bureaucracies can be, and how subject to corruption.

An old family friend who worked for the town of Thetford helped guide Tom into the civil service. Tom had to supply his birth certificate, get letters of recommendation from influential people on good terms with the government, and swear an oath that he had not paid off anyone to advance his application.

Months later, an Excise supervisor came by to check Tom's health and intelligence, his personal habits, and his handwriting ability. Tom also had to prove he was free of debt, was loyal to the government, and was a recognized member of the Church of England.

These hurdles leaped, Tom took lessons from the local exciseman on how to measure casks of all shapes and sizes and record the results in a notebook. Next came a formal examination by the supervisor. It tested Tom's English, his arithmetic skills, and his proficiency in all the paperwork the job required. Passing these tests, Tom then had to get two people to stand as security: they had to pledge to pay the government two hundred pounds—a lot of money!—in case Tom mishandled the taxes he would collect on the job.

Clearly corruption was a serious concern of the government. In a job collecting tax money, a man paid miserably low wages might be easily tempted to skim off some of that money for himself. And every bit of that cash was vital to a government that needed huge sums for its daily operations and its long-term stability.

Tom got a lesson in how knowing people in the right places worked. Through the man who guided him in his first steps, and probably through the Duke of Grafton, the region's most powerful figure, a commissioner in the Excise Office was reached, who arranged for Tom's appointment to go through. That kind of deal was common; many jobs were obtained that way (and still are).

But still more was called for before he could begin work. He had to swear an oath that he would do his job faithfully, another that he would never accept any fee for services other than from the government, another that he had taken the Sacrament in the parish church. And finally, and most importantly, he had to take the Oath of Supremacy. He swore that King George III was the lawful king of England and that no pretenders to the throne had Paine's allegiance. (No one would have guessed that one day Tom would call for rebellion against the monarchy.)

At last, in December 1762, fourteen months after he began the long process, a letter came telling him to start work in Grantham, in Lincolnshire. He began as an apprentice officer, at the junior level. His job was to gauge the brewer's casks, limited and boring work giving him little chance to learn other tasks that would advance his career. In August 1764 he was promoted to a better job, collecting revenues at Alford.

The new position was better for him in one sense but worse in another. For almost everyone dislikes paying taxes, and the people of Alford despised the local excise taxes on the everyday articles they consumed. Alford was close by the North Sea coast, an area notorious for smug-

Part of Paine's job as an exciseman was to patrol for smugglers, here attacked by the King's soldiers.

gling. Armed gangs made deals with seamen bringing in casks of a popular Dutch gin. Smuggling in the cargo, they bypassed the exciseman. Part of Tom's job was to patrol the coast on horseback, watching out for ships and smugglers, alerting the town constable to their movements.

Despite the government's efforts, huge amounts of goods were smuggled in and out of the country. Both small traders and consumers resented the taxes and the harsh measures taken to halt the illegal trade.

Capture of a smuggler meant death by hanging. In nearby towns smugglers retaliated by beating up excisemen or wrecking their offices, often with the quiet approval of the neighbors.

Luckily, Paine never suffered physical harm. But the bitterness of the people must have eaten into his spirit. Here he was, a royal officer, enjoying a secure profession, while all around him were people struggling to fend off poverty. How did it feel to do work that his "clients" hated and resisted?

Many excisemen allowed goods that should have been taxed to pass through without assessment. Instead of examining the merchandise, they accepted whatever value the owner placed on it, and then stamped the excise tax papers accordingly. The practice, called stamping, was a way to avoid angering the traders. Some officers did not even go to the traders' offices to examine the goods but took bribes to write up false reports.

A year after he started work, Paine was accused of stamping by his supervisor and fired from the service. Studying the records, biographer John Keane suggests Paine was framed by his supervisor, who himself avoided being fired for misconduct by making false charges against the new man, confident that the top authorities almost always closed ranks against the bottom dogs.

Again, Paine's life was broken up. This time not by natural causes but by the unjust act of a despotic government. Long ago, in Thetford, he had witnessed how cruelly the orders of a king, the laws of Parliament, and the decisions of judges operated against people without power.

Where did that power reside? Who exercised it? And in whose interests? What determined the division between the rulers and the ruled?

In childhood Tom had grown aware of who held the power in his own community. It was the noble Grafton family, the Dukes of Grafton, who lived in the vast brick palace called Euston Hall. Their immense estate was nearly forty miles in circumference. It embraced many villages as well as Thetford. The Graftons were part of a very small class of landed rich. They all agreed that property was the very foundation of civilization and that only those who held property were fit to rule. By constantly acquiring more and more land, through purchase and marriage, families like the Graftons piled up more and more wealth, while the agricultural laborers who worked their estate sank deeper and deeper into poverty.

The Graftons, like the other aristocrats, operated a great system of patronage. Their rule over the county was almost absolute. They handed out salaried jobs, rented out farmland, assigned licenses and building contracts. They watched over and controlled the community's public life.

Elections for public officer were a joke by democratic standards. The right to vote was very narrowly limited to property holders of a certain standing. Thetford sent two members to Parliament, but only thirty voters elected them. Elections were, therefore, almost never contested. The chosen ones were either members of the duke's own family or were men completely obedient to their wishes. The right to elect members to Parliament had no relation to the distribution of the population or the size of a town.

Eighteenth-century Britain did not believe in democracy. The world of authority belonged to owners of property and not to the dispossessed. For most of the century, until Tom Paine did much to incite change, there was little protest against the way the political machine worked in favor of the very rich.

George III, ruler of Paine's Britain.

The king provided the great majority of places in the government for those loyal to him. He appointed all ministers and dismissed them at will. They were dependent on him for their powers. Members of Parliament were pledged only to very broad political principles. There were no specific planks of a party program they were bound to support.

The king and the court were at the heart of political and social life. The Georges—of the house of Hanover, who began to rule over Britain in 1714—were "both stupid and obstinate," says British historian J. H. Plumb, "and they could not grasp the complexities of either foreign or domestic affairs. Nevertheless, great as the Crown's powers were, Britain was a constitutional monarchy, and the only one in the world."

Under the terms of the Magna Carta the king could not be a Roman Catholic, he could not suspend the laws, and he had to depend on Parliament for his income and his armed forces. "In the final reckoning," said Plumb, "power was not with him but with Parliament." Yet government had to depend on the King's goodwill, whether the government's policies were popular with the public or not.

The way in which Tom lost his excise job gave him a personal taste of how government operated to protect the favored few. Though the Crown boasted of Britain as the home of liberty and good government, he realized how hollow that claim was. But what could he do about it?

At twenty-eight, he found himself once again dependent upon his parents. He went back to Thetford and with the help of his father's friends got work as a journeyman corset maker in Diss, a small town fifteen miles from Thetford. He floundered about, unable to focus on his work, irritable, sick of his trade, driven by a sense of hopelessness.

Again he appealed to his father. Mr. Paine's friend, the town official who had helped once before, pulled strings at the Excise Board to have Tom's job restored. Tom went to London and, stuffing his pride in his pocket, humbly begged for reinstatement, all the while knowing that behind the scenes a deal was being made. Probably someone with power was being paid "to do the right thing." In July 1766, the Excise Board ordered that Paine be reinstated when the proper vacancy occurred.

When that would happen, no one knew. Meanwhile Tom found other work, teaching reading and writing in a private school for working-class children. It was run by a Methodist preacher, David Noble, who was known as a dissenter and an advocate for civil liberties. This was one of several new schools established to help working-class boys (and sometimes girls) acquire skills in arithmetic, the use of English, bookkeeping, and technical drawing. Tom's pay was only half his salary as an excise officer and scarcely enough for even a single man to live on.

The energy of London life, however, refreshed his mind and spirit. He got in touch with the scientists who had done so much before to broaden his understanding of the world. "I have seldom passed five minutes of my life,

Paine is unlikely to have brutalized his working-class pupils the way this English schoolmaster did in this caricature by George Cruikshank.

however circumstanced," he said, "in which I did not acquire some knowledge."

That knowledge Paine spread to others. Now and then he would go out to London's open fields to preach the Methodist gospel. Listening to more experienced lay preachers, he sharpened his skills in the use of vivid everyday language as he spoke to the crowds' concern for social justice.

These were the years of rapidly accelerating economic and social change in Britain. London became a modern metropolis as both population and wealth grew. The artisans like those Tom was teaching provided a large reading public for the newspapers. Even in the provincial towns the people had begun to debate political questions. Among these was the cause of the American colonies, which by this time were showing signs of rebellion against imperial control. Conversation clubs had sprung up in many places. They moved toward political action by passing resolutions and sending critical letters to the press. Many supported John Wilkes, a political reformer and newspaper publisher who openly attacked the Crown and its policies.

No one with a lively mind, living in London then, could fail to be affected by its ferment. The superb wit of Wilkes, the rebel politician, must have fortified Paine's belief that something needed to be done to bring about greater social justice.

Then, in February 1768, the Excise Office sent Tom to work in the Sussex town of Lewes.

❖ 4 ❖
A Writer's Beginnings

From learning about politics in London, Tom would turn to political action in Lewes. The town, about twice the size of Thetford, was a lively marketing center. It had a thriving social life, boasting a cricket team, circulating library, bowling society, debating clubs, and a visiting theater company. It also had a long tradition of opposition politics, dating back to the English Revolution of the 1640s, when the Puritan majority in Lewes elected two radicals to Parliament. After the fall of the Commonwealth and the return of the monarchy, many of the stubborn Quakers had been jailed. Yet punishment never squelched the nonconformists.

Tom rented lodgings above the tobacco shop of Samuel and Esther Ollive, Methodists with three sons and a daughter, Elizabeth. The Ollives were drawn to the new excise officer, with his skill on skates and horseback, his quick mind, and his great interest in public affairs. The local government was again in the hands of republic-minded citizens, a body known as the Society of Twelve. Samuel Ollive, Tom's landlord, was one of them, and he soon arranged for Tom to be co-opted to membership.

Tom took part in the society's meetings, during which the members debated what to do about all sorts of public issues. He enjoyed his first taste of local self-government. He also went to vestry meetings of St. Michael's Church. The vestry levied local parish taxes and discussed how to use them to meet local needs, including small weekly payments to orphans, widows, and the poor.

During the six years Paine stayed in Lewes he was active in the Headstrong Club, a group of civic-minded people that met weekly in the White Hart Inn. After a mug of ale and a dish of oysters, the circle argued about national and international issues, as well as local ones.

Paine was said to be the best debater in the club, "a shrewd and sensible fellow" with a deep knowledge of politics. Such praise made him so cocky that he was accused of conceit (an accusation that followed him all his life).

It was in Lewes that he first showed considerable skill in writing. He published several pieces in the local newspaper (signing one "Common Sense") that defended freedom of the press. Other pieces offered a design for a new kind of fire escape or denounced the cruel abuse of vagabonds. He tried his hand at satire, too. One of these pieces denounced religious bigotry, and another attacked the power of the aristocratic ruling class. Unlike Tom, many people believed poverty was "a most necessary and indisputable ingredient in society." Even reformers in that day thought the gulf between rich and poor could never be overcome. It was only natural to defer to the rich, just as wives were expected to defer to husbands. But it wasn't natural or inevitable to Paine. He spoke against and wrote against that kind of conservative dogma with passionate tongue and pen.

Probably much debate in the Headstrong Club centered on the growing crisis in the American colonies. The Boston Massacre occurred in 1770, when a crowd led by the Sons of Liberty gathered to confront British soldiers guarding the Custom House. Someone threw snowballs, the soldiers panicked, and shots were fired, killing five colonists and wounding several others. The American radicals saw this as a chilling example of the British threat to liberty.

Later, in 1773, news of the Boston Tea Party reached Lewes. Three British ships carrying cargoes of tea had anchored in Boston Harbor, but the colonials demanded they go back to England without the Americans paying any

When news of the Boston Massacre of 1770 reached Paine's political club in Lewes, it encouraged dissent against the Crown's colonial policy.

duty. When Britain's colonial governor refused to permit it, a group of men disguised as Mohawk Indians boarded the ships and threw the tea into the harbor.

That event enraged King George. But there were some who were not afraid to disagree with his colonial policy, and dissenters in Lewes and many other places were among them. John Wilkes was a spokesman for them; the local newspaper, the *Lewes Journal*, praised him as a "great patriot." When he came to Lewes, Wilkes was given a hero's welcome. He visited the Headstrong Club, where Paine may have met him.

Wilkes appealed to the people for support in his fight against political corruption. He took advantage of the popular feeling that Parliament was not for them, and certainly not of them, and rallied public feeling behind his cause. Tom wanted answers to the big questions Wilkes raised: What rights did the people of England have? In

John Wilkes, radical journalist and politician, whose championship of popular rights inspired Paine.

what way were their basic needs met by the government? How could they make their will felt in London, when every part of government was closed to them?

These, Tom learned from the newspapers, were the same questions the Americans were demanding answers to. And just as with the Headstrong Club, the Americans were forming extraparliamentary organizations to press for political reform.

Meanwhile Tom's personal life took a turn when his friend and landlord, Samuel Ollive, died. Mrs. Ollive asked Paine to help run the family shop, even though he had no aptitude for business ventures. Tom drew close to her daughter, Elizabeth, a bright young woman who had just launched a school for girls. On March 26, 1771, they married. He was thirty-four, and his wife, twenty-one.

But family happiness didn't last long. Business at the store fell off badly, and Tom's excise pay was too low to provide decent support. Besides, his work took him on the road for long stretches, adding to the strain on the family. Only a year after the marriage they had to sell everything they owned at auction just to survive.

Bitter quarrels broke out between Tom and Elizabeth, and soon they decided to separate. Divorce was very rare—it took a private Act of Parliament to obtain one—and the Paines never were divorced. (Elizabeth lived on until 1808, dying just a year before Paine.) The wife was considered disgraced in such circumstances, and Elizabeth moved away from Lewes, never to return. She went to live with a brother and managed to scrape by as a dressmaker. From time to time Paine would send her some money, anonymously, but they never met again. It was a terrible time for women, who had almost no rights under the law. A wife was "as much a man's property as his horse," wrote the early feminist, Mary Wollstonecraft.

As shaken as he must have been, Tom managed to keep working. But his dissatisfaction with his job would soon lead him to produce his first major piece of writing: a plea for social justice.

❖ 5 ❖

OUT OF A JOB

T he struggle of his own family to survive pushed Paine into political pamphleteering. All families of excisemen suffered in the same way. In 1772 some excise officers asked him to present their case for better wages and working conditions to Parliament. They agreed the plan had to be carried out in secret, as it was illegal for employees of the Crown to organize into what was in effect a trade union.

This was Paine's first cause and he threw himself into it with the same passion that he would later bring to the American and French revolutions. For several weeks he collected evidence and prepared a petition. Then, taking leave from his job, he went to London to lobby members of Parliament. He handed out to them his twenty-one page pamphlet headed *The Case of the Officers of Excise.*

The Case was carefully written and well argued. Paine showed that while the excisemen had to endure long hours, hard work, and separation from their families, they were paid miserably low wages. On humane grounds alone they deserved a salary increase.

But he did more. He described how the wretched poverty the officers suffered led to corruption. It is a natural principle for people to do anything not to starve, he argued. And because their occupation offered opportunities to defraud the government, it followed that dishonesty was the almost "inevitable consequence of poverty." Raise our pay, he pleaded, and it will "produce more good effect than all the laws of the land can enforce." The excisemen would benefit from increased pay, and the government would benefit from increased revenues as corruption disappeared.

Paine didn't portray the excisemen as saints in a sinful world. He was honest and blunt in showing how they were trapped by the system they had become a part of. Graft, tips, bribes, payoffs—yes, this was corruption—but none of it was inherent in human nature. People were not naturally bad, he was saying; the wrongs they committed were the product of poverty. Abolish the poverty by raising pay, and corruption would cease.

In creating his pamphlet Paine used an approach that would work to great effect in his later writings. He established the facts of the case and then advanced a principle to explain the consequences of those facts. And finally he recommended new policies that would fit the principle and improve everyone's situation.

He wrote in clear, direct, convincing style. He did not appeal to authority or precedent or inflate his prose with scholarly citations. He grounded his case on practical experience. Like the scientists he had learned from, he insisted on the supremacy of the facts.

The pamphlet voiced his social views: sympathy for the poor, dislike of great wealth. There is a hint of the need for deeper change, of the kind he would favor one day soon in America.

Personally, it was a time of despair. What had he done with his thirty-seven years? Why had he failed in everything? He had neither wife nor children nor money nor property. All he had was a certain talent with words, but a talent thus far barely used. How, where could he make a fresh start? Was that new land, America, the place for him?

He went back to London, where he managed to get an appointment to see Benjamin Franklin. No man was better known in all Europe. An agent of the Pennsylvania colony, he was experiencing great difficulty dealing with the mother country. But always affable, he set aside time for this nobody, Tom Paine.

Paine knew the scientific work that had won the older man great fame. And he knew as well that Franklin

Benjamin Franklin, who opened doors to America for Paine, was among the many Founding Fathers painted by the portraitist Charles Willson Peale.

believed the Crown was sorely testing the colonies' loyalty. Seeing something of value in Paine, Franklin gave him a letter of introduction to his son-in-law, a merchant in Philadelphia, asking him to give Paine "your best advice" and to help him to find work. At that very moment the First Continental Congress, meeting at Philadelphia, had decided to cut off all trade with Britain in retaliation against its colonial policy and announced that it would not abide by Parliament's laws or the king's word when it infringed upon their liberties.

With Franklin's letter in his pocket, Paine felt this was his chance to make a new start in life. At the end of September 1774, he boarded a ship bound for America.

❖ 6 ❖

LOVE AFFAIR WITH AMERICA

Paine came close to never reaching America alive. His ship, the *London Packet*, sailed with 120 passengers aboard, most of them indentured servants from England or Germany. An epidemic of typhus raged through the decks, infecting all but seven passengers. Five died, their bodies tossed into the sea. Paine was so sick with the "putrid fever" he had to be carried off the ship on a stretcher when it docked at Philadelphia on November 30, 1774. A doctor, told that Paine came recommended by Franklin, took care of the nearly dead man for six weeks until he recovered.

When Paine felt better, he gave Richard Bache, the husband of Franklin's daughter, the letter of introduction. He rented a room at the corner of Market and Front streets, close by the auction shed of the slave market. Next door to Paine was Robert Aitkin's bookshop, which had one of the largest collections of books in the colony and a printing press in the rear. Aitkin soon noticed the thin tall man with graying brown hair who dropped in often to browse the shelves. His casual conversations with this unknown Englishman impressed Aitkin, himself a recent immigrant from Scotland. Paine was so knowledgeable and talked so well!

Aitkin was about to launch a new monthly periodical, to be called the *Pennsylvania Magazine*. Maybe this Englishman could edit it? After seeing some of Paine's writings, Aitkin offered him the job. It would pay fifty pounds a year, not a lot but enough to get by on. Aitkin would control policy while Paine would handle the daily editing chores.

While waiting for the magazine to be launched, Paine looked around the town. Philadelphia had been founded and planned about a hundred years earlier by the English Quaker William Penn. It had become America's largest city and busiest port. Its population of some thirty thousand was very varied: Quakers, Anglicans, Catholics of English descent, Lutherans and Mennonites from Germany, and Scotch-Irish Presbyterians.

Although it bragged of being "the capital of the new world," the town covered less than a square mile. But it had reason to boast, for it was the financial and commercial center of the colonies. The arts, theater, schools, philanthropic institutions all flourished there. And interest in science, so dear to Tom's heart, was as intense as in London. Here, too, he could attend popular lectures on scientific advances.

The state house in Philadelphia, where the first Continental Congress was meeting at the time Paine arrived in town.

Much of the working force was made up of involuntary labor. There were six hundred slaves, nine hundred indentured servants, and many apprentices in 1775. The free lower class, swollen by constant immigration, was comprised mostly of sailors, dock workers, hired servants, and unskilled laborers.

The city's artisans and laborers had a long history of fighting poverty, unemployment, and rising prices. These self-educated mechanics had formed their own organization and recently, as relations with Britain soured, had begun to hold political meetings and to put forward their own candidates for office.

Political power had long been in the hands of the merchant aristocracy. It dominated local government as well as social and economic life. By the time Paine arrived in Philadelphia the richest 10 percent owned half the city's wealth; the poorest 40 percent owned only 4 percent of the wealth (a contrast not unlike the gap that separates the rich from the poor in America today). With wealth went a haughty superiority. The rich treated the working people below them with what some critics called "surly pride" and "insulting rudeness."

The merchants traded farm products, supplied imports to storekeepers, and extended credit to rural customers. Their commerce dominated the lives of all Philadelphians; the artisans and laborers were dependent upon them. If the merchants did not do well, then everyone else soon felt the effects.

And there was no guarantee they would do well. Even the wealthiest merchants were sometimes at the mercy of decisions made thousands of miles away by Britain's Parliament.

If not by affection, artisans and merchants were tied together by commerce. The artisans had to rely on the merchants for credit and access to capital. Merchants controlled the supplies artisans needed—wood, hides, iron—and merchants were the main buyers of craft products. But more and more artisans came to see that British insistence on supplying the colonies with all their manufactured goods was a threat to their own economic well-being. They became economic nationalists, pressing for agreements not to import British goods.

Yet the artisans were not interested solely in making money. Most worked in their own homes and answered to no one but themselves for the hours they put in or the quality of work they turned out. They usually did every task involved in making a finished product. They took breaks in the workday whenever they liked. That control over their own time meant much to them. Unlike the common laborers who worked for employers, they could make time to be active in the cultural and social life of the community, as well as in its politics.

The sensitive Paine had quickly felt the great upheaval shaking the earth beneath his feet:

> *I happened to come to America a few months before the breaking out of hostilities. The world could not then have persuaded me that I should be either a soldier or an author. But when the country, into which I had just set my foot, was set on fire about my ears, it was time to stir. It was time for every man to stir.*

Yet at first Paine was not eager to plunge into colonial politics. As he said later, "All the plans or prospects of private life (for I am not by nature fond of, or fitted for a public one and feel all occasions of it where I must act personally a burden), all these plans, I say, were immediately disconcerted, and I was at once involved in all the troubles of the country."

He had no material self-interest in taking part, for he had neither money nor property to protect. He became active purely on principle.

The war was just around the corner. In Massachusetts the provincial congress took steps to prepare the colony to fight. Americans would no longer submit to the dictates of British power. Late in January 1775 the first issue of the

Pennsylvania Magazine appeared. It carried the full text of the petition of the Continental Congress to King George III. The world was moving forward and upward, Paine assured his readers. And he looked to America to keep it rolling. It was a sign that his love affair with his newly adopted land had begun. The magazine was a miscellany of articles on such subjects as a cure for typhus, the habits of beavers, a new electricity generator, probably some written by Paine. (As was the custom, contributions were anonymous or signed with pen names.) There were brief reports on world events and letters from correspondents in America and Europe.

This began Paine's literary apprenticeship. He experimented with different ways and forms of writing. He dealt with the ideas of contributors who challenged his own thinking. And he found that his ideas counted.

During his editorship Paine published perhaps two dozen pieces in the magazine. Some of his work dealt with developments in science and technology. He wrote poems and satires, too. As his pieces flowed out, they showed signs of creative growth, says his biographer John Keane, "a new Paine of crisp, lean, lightning-quick sentences, hammering out political point after point for an audience of self-educated artisans and ordinary folk like himself, for whom reading and being read to were new and exhilarating experiences."

And that was what Paine wanted above all: to make his words count, to encourage citizens to think, speak, and act with confidence in themselves and their beliefs. "The public," he said, "may justly be called the true fountain of honor." His own writings rallied new readers to the magazine. It had begun with about six hundred subscribers, but in a few months the number jumped to more than fifteen hundred, making it the best-selling periodical published in America. His new career was fixed. For the first time in his life, he was a success.

One reader impressed by Paine's writing was the young Philadelphia physician Benjamin Rush. Browsing in Aitkin's bookshop one day, Rush met Paine. They shared a

Benjamin Rush, Philadelphia physician and member of the Continental Congress, was one of Paine's first friends in America.

strong interest in social and political affairs and quickly became friends. Soon after their first conversation, Rush was excited by an essay in the *Pennsylvania Magazine* denouncing slavery.

Years before, in 1769, Rush had written: "It would be useless for us to denounce the servitude to which the Parliament of Great Britain wishes to reduce us, while we continue to keep our fellow creatures in slavery just because their color is different from ours." A few years later Rush published a pamphlet calling slavery "a national crime."

No thinking or feeling person could ignore the half million slaves scattered throughout the colonies. The greatest numbers were on the rice and tobacco plantations of the South. In Philadelphia many slaves worked side by side with apprentices and servants in the workshops of artisans. Others worked in the taverns or the shipyards. Living close by the auction block where newly arrived slaves were sold to the highest bidders, Paine was appalled and disgusted by what he saw. Pick up any newspaper and you would see advertisements offering rewards for the capture and return of runaway slaves. So he decided to write "African Slavery in America." In his essay Paine asked how is it consistent, or decent, for Americans "to complain so loudly of attempts to enslave them, while they hold so many hundreds of thousands in slavery, and annually enslave many thousands more?" He pointed out:

> Too many nations enslaved the prisoners they took in war. But to go to nations with whom there is no war, who have no way provoked, without farther design of conquest, purely to catch inoffensive people, like the wild beasts, for slaves, is an height of outrage against humanity and justice, that seems left by heathen nations to be practised by pretended Christians. How shameful are all attempts to colour and excuse it!
>
> As these people are not convicted for forfeiting freedom, they have still a natural, perfect right to it; and the governments whenever they come should, in justice set them free, and punish those who hold them in slavery.
>
> So monstrous is the making and keeping them slaves at all, abstracted from the barbarous usage they suffer, and the many evils attending the practice; as selling husbands away from wives, children from parents, and from each other, in violation of sacred and natural ties; and opening the way for adulteries, incests, and many shocking consequences, for all of which the guilty masters must answer to the final judge.

If the slavery of the parents be unjust, much more is their children's; if the parents were justly slaves, yet the children are born free; this is the natural, perfect right of all mankind; they are nothing but a just recompense to those who bring them up: And as much less is commonly spent on them than others, they have a right, in justice, to be proportionately sooner free.

Certainly one may, with as much reason and decency, plead for murder, robbery, lewdness, and barbarity, as for this practice. They are not more contrary to the natural dictates of conscience, and feelings of humanity; nay, they are all comprehended in it.

Paine labeled slaveowners as thieves and argued that the slave, who was the proper owner of his freedom, had a right to reclaim it. Slavery, he held, was the one blot on America's character. He wanted the colonists to realize the full implications of their demand for liberty and extend it to all people regardless of race.

The publication of that essay on March 8, 1775, strengthened Paine's growing reputation for liberal views. It won for him the friendship not only of Dr. Rush but of other leaders in the colonial resistance to Britain. Ironically, Britain was in advance of America on this issue. There were about 10,000 slaves in England when Chief Justice Mansfield, in 1772, made his famous judgment in the case of the slave Somerset, declaring slavery illegal in England. (Parliament would abolish the slave trade itself in 1806.)

A few months after the antislavery essay, Paine published his first political poem, "Liberty Tree." It portrayed America as a land of equality, brotherhood, and freedom, trying to protect itself from an aggressive Britain. The "tyranny" of Britain he blamed on everyone with power—the king, his ministers, and the Parliament—thus building the foundation for a movement toward independence. He gave hearty support to the declaration of the Continental Congress that if Americans wanted freedom, they must be prepared to fight for it.

Paine was held back from expressing some of his views because Aitkin did not want to antagonize any wealthy subscribers who feared the more radical wing of the revolutionary movement. Many Americans, like Paine himself for a time, felt it possible to negotiate the colonies' differences with England. But the explosive impact of just one event showed how hopeless was that outlook.

It happened on April 19, 1775. Blood was spilled in Massachusetts when a British general sent a thousand troops to Concord to capture munitions hidden by farmers and village people organized as "minutemen." Resisted by the Americans as they passed through Lexington, the British troops regrouped and marched on to Concord. At the bridge crossing the Concord River the redcoats met the gunfire of angry colonials. There were dead and wounded on both sides, and the British retreated.

The Battle of Lexington in April 1775, the explosive event that convinced Paine compromise with Britain was useless.

Express riders carrying the news of Lexington and Concord blazed through New England, down the coast to Georgia, and westward across the mountains. The Second Continental Congress met in Philadelphia in May 1775 with a war on its hands. It had to raise an army, funds, and supplies. As the troops of nearby colonies moved up to Boston to aid in its defense, the Congress unanimously chose George Washington to be commander-in-chief of a Continental army.

The battle of Lexington and Concord convinced Paine that all proposals to settle the differences with Britain by compromise were useless now. He knew that many of the artisans and laborers of Philadelphia felt the same as did the farmers in the rural districts. But were the rich merchant aristocrats ready to struggle for independence? They feared that out of it might come a republic, a new government that would crush their privilege and authority. They still hoped to make some sort of deal that would preserve their power.

What could Tom Paine do about it? I'm determined, he said, "to change the sentiments of the people from dependence to independence and from the monarchial to the republican form of government."

But how?

❖ 7 ❖
MASTER
PROPAGANDIST

In issue after issue of the *Pennsylvania Magazine* Paine fired off shots against Britain. Britain was nothing but a "plunderer," he charged, an "invader," a kind of political highwayman holding up America. The colonists were used to thinking of England as the "mother" country. Paine tried to break down that image by claiming that this parent was "red with the blood of her children."

He bombarded readers with attacks upon kings and aristocrats. He seized on Britain's long rule over India to illustrate how ruthless and corrupt the Empire was in exploiting a subject people. He attacked the honors given those who held titles. Lord? Duke? Marquis? King? Such people ought to get only what they deserve. A king, he said, should be awarded the title of "Honorable plunderer of his country, or the Right Honorable murderer of mankind."

In everything he wrote he criticized Old World life as backward and unjust. But this New World of his adoption, he said, was committed to progress and liberty. He wrote with a double advantage: He could see each world in the light of his experience with the other world. The very fact that he had suffered the harsh restrictions of England made him want to turn America into the land of liberty.

Paine was becoming a master of revolutionary propaganda. People tend to think of propaganda as evil, its methods dangerous, its results harmful. Look at it objectively. What is it? A tool, an instrument, that can be used for good or evil. Students of social psychology agree that it is a systematic attempt by one or more persons to shape the attitudes of groups of people through the use of suggestion, with the aim of affecting their actions.

Propagandists are trying to obtain public support for a particular idea or course of action. That in itself is not harmful. What may be questioned is the technique a particular propagandist uses. It isn't necessary for the propaganda to be false or for the propagandist to conceal his or her motive.

You can see propaganda used everywhere you look today—in advertising and publicity campaigns, in elections, in diplomatic maneuvers, in international crises. There is nothing new about it. All human history illustrates how people trying to promote a course of action use various means to win public support by suggestion. Where absolute monarchs or dictators hold power, they have less need of this tool. But the more democratic a community, the greater the need for rallying public opinion.

To get large bodies of people to cooperate in as complex a movement as striving for a revolutionary change in society, molding public opinion is essential. In the American Revolution as in all revolutions its leaders had to use propaganda widely and effectively. If the Revolution had been launched by a majority, with everyone agreed on methods and goals, there would have been much less need for propaganda.

But that was not the case. Although there had long been conditions dividing England from the colonies and tendencies toward separation had grown since the early 1760s, in 1775 there was still serious disagreement among the colonists.

That seems incredible to us today. Here you had the colonies in a state of open warfare with England, yet no one had publicly made an appeal for independence. The Continental Congress, an illegal body in British eyes, had made itself the supreme authority in the land. It ran military affairs and negotiated with foreign powers. Yet the moderates in the congress were still saying they wanted nothing more than to have their grievances settled. Even the radical congressmen were not asking for independence; they didn't want to alienate the more conservative or timid members.

Some groups believed preserving the union with Britain held solid benefits. Others feared that the separate colonies, with varying interests and quarrelsome governments, would not be able to unite against the most powerful empire in the world.

At every stage of the developing conflict the leaders met great difficulties. Thousands of Tories, who opposed the Revolution, suffered violence or were forced into exile. Many other leaders remained sullenly or timorously in control, or indifferent. Even among the top leadership there was frequent dissension that hampered action. Most historians agree that "the Revolution was at best the work of an aggressive minority."

So propaganda was vital to those who first called for resistance to Britain and then launched a revolution. In the fall of 1775 Paine wrote, "I hesitate not for a moment to

This line drawing of Thomas Paine was published in England in 1791.

believe that the Almighty will finally separate America from Britain. Call it Independence or what you will, if it is the cause of God and humanity it will go on."

Paine was not alone in thinking this. Benjamin Rush was already urging people privately that America ought to establish an independent republic. But Paine would go public. He began work on a pamphlet that would argue the case for American separation from Britain. He was worried over the fears and hesitations expressed by some delegates to the Continental Congress. His own Pennsylvania Assembly had just instructed its delegates to vote against independence if the issue came up. He hoped his pamphlet would influence Americans to use their common sense and make the final break with Britain.

Why a pamphlet? Remember that there were almost no other ways to reach a broad public in that time. No radio, no television, no film, no electronic "information

Town meetings were the scene of fierce debate over the issue of resistance to Britain. A scene by John Trumbull, painter of American's revolutionary history.

highway." That made the press a most essential part of everyday life. Most of the papers were weeklies (there were no dailies), and there were only about three dozen of them in all the colonies. The news that they printed was largely political, both foreign and domestic.

People believed in a "free press," but they didn't see it the way we do now. Editors favoring the resistance to Britain—and there were far more of them than editors opposed to revolution—saw freedom as the right to express their own beliefs as against those that were loyal to the king. They thought it was all right to suppress the opposing views. In Boston a publisher of a Tory paper was beaten up so badly by a mob that he fled the colony. There were some editors who believed freedom of the press meant newspapers should publish any opinion on public issues. But others were like Benjamin Franklin, who said he ran a newspaper to suit himself. It anyone wanted to voice conflicting views, they could do it through a pamphlet. And he was ready to run it off on his printing press—if paid for it.

So pamphleteering became a major method of reaching the public. As Paine began to make notes for his pamphlet, the refusal of Aitkin, the publisher of the *Pennsylvania Magazine*, to raise his pay led Paine to quit the job. Neglecting all else, he plunged into the writing of what would become the bible of the movement for independence.

❖ 8 ❖

COMMON SENSE

Governments go to war for all kinds of reasons. In a war fought by professional soldiers, highly disciplined troops usually obey the order to fight that comes from above. But a civil war is fought by amateurs—volunteers—and they need powerful moral reasons to risk their lives. The American Revolution was really a civil war, our first civil war. If there were to be enough patriots to overthrow Britain's rule, then popular enthusiasm for the war had to be heated to the boiling point.

That was what Tom Paine set out to do. A writer who had both the brains and the passion, he produced one of the great gems of propaganda literature. In a crisis of great confusion, his pamphlet had the very appealing title *Common Sense*. It appeared on January 10, 1776, and within almost no time it exhausted the printers and presses of the colonies. In a population of only three million, people bought hundreds of thousands of copies, creating America's first best-seller.

Why was *Common Sense* so effective? Because Paine recognized what was needed: not an attack on this British policy or that but a radical change in America's understanding of what the British Empire was and meant. Paine wanted to demolish the whole framework of British thought within which Americans had lived—the subordination expected of them, the deference to monarchy, the reverence for the British constitution.

Paine realized what was troubling most people. Pamphleteers before him had attacked the British Parliament, blamed it for the burden of oppressive taxation, and wiped out any expectation that those men in London would change policy and lift their burdens.

But there was still the great symbol of authority that stood far above the Parliament. And that was the Crown. The more Parliament was attacked, the tighter people clung to the hope that the king would rescue the colonies. The fear of letting go the hope was desperate and widespread. The king was an age-old symbol of authority and power, somehow linked to God ("the divine right of kings")—a symbol terribly hard to destroy.

Yet Paine knew it had to be destroyed. And more, he believed that many Americans unconsciously wished to be rid of it. One of his goals in writing *Common Sense* was to demolish monarchy as a sacred institution. Another was to demolish King George III himself.

He developed his argument carefully in four parts. He asked, how did governments originate, and what was their design? The purpose of government was to provide freedom and security, he said. "And however our eyes may be dazzled with show, or our ears deceived by sound; however prejudice may warp our wills, or interest darken our understanding, the simple voice of nature and reason will say, 'tis right.'"

As for the design of government, he wrote: "I draw my idea of the form of government from a principle in nature which no art can overturn—that the more simple anything is, the less liable it is to be disordered, and the easier repaired when disordered."

With these basic premises in mind, Paine examined the "much boasted constitution of England." He showed it was not only "exceedingly complex" but also "imperfect, subject to convulsions, and incapable of providing what it seems to promise." He did this to tear down the respect for the British constitution, which hampered a rational view of its nature and real-life effects. Once you saw how irrational that constitution was, you could then plan a government by the simple principles of reason and nature.

In the second part of *Common Sense* Paine took up monarchy. Because people "were originally equals in the order of creation," how could kings come into the world "so

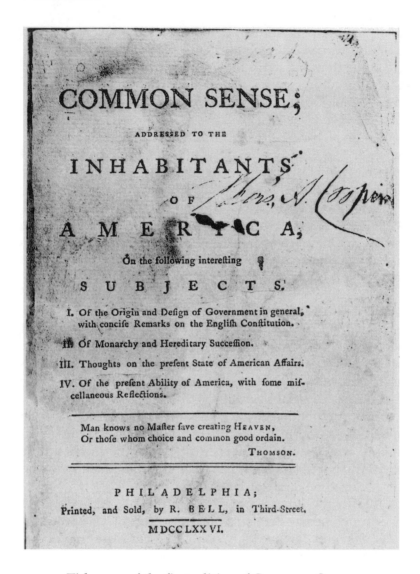

COMMON SENSE;

ADDRESSED TO THE

INHABITANTS

OF

AMERICA,

On the following interefting

SUBJECTS.

I. Of the Origin and Defign of Government in general,
with concife Remarks on the Englifh Conftitution.

II. Of Monarchy and Hereditary Succeffion.

III. Thoughts on the prefent State of American Affairs.

IV. Of the prefent Ability of America, with fome mif-
cellaneous Reflections.

Man knows no Mafter fave creating HEAVEN,
Or thofe whom choice and common good ordain.
THOMSON.

PHILADELPHIA;

Printed, and Sold, by R. BELL, in Third-Street.

MDCCLXXVI.

Title page of the first edition of Common Sense,
Paine's masterwork.

exalted above the rest?" Is anything more absurd than the
hereditary principle? Paine said later, "as absurd as an
hereditary mathematician, or an hereditary wise man and

as ridiculous as an hereditary poet-laureate?" Paine encouraged his readers to look at the practical effects of hereditary monarchy. Are kings "the means of happiness or of misery to mankind?" The traditional view of hereditary succession was that it provided peace and stability. But that was nonsense. In England alone, he asserted, the monarchy had produced "no less than eight civil wars and nineteen rebellions" and has laid the world in "blood and ashes."

Now that he had tried to break America's faith in England's constitution and monarchy, Paine took up the immediate issues troubling Americans in the early months of 1776. To his reader he would "offer nothing more than simple truths, plain arguments and common sense."

Making the case for independence, he considered and rejected the chief arguments for reconciliation with Britain. To those who believed America's prosperity and security depended upon union with Britain, he replied that America "would have flourished as much, and probably more, had no European power taken any notice of her." And further, Britain only got the colonies entangled in the quarrels of Europe. As for the sentimental notion that Britain was the mother country, Paine snorted that "even brutes do not devour their young." And he pointed out that "the persecuted lovers of civil and religious liberty" had fled "not from the tender embraces of the mother, but from the cruelty of the monster."

Could Britain be persuaded to treat the colonies with justice? No, Paine replied; "America is not the main concern of British politics. Britain's own self-interest leads her to suppress the colonies' interest whenever it does not promote her own advantage."

To sum up the issue, he asked, "Is the power who is jealous of our prosperity, a proper power to govern us? Whoever says No to this question, is an Independent."

But would the winning of independence be enough? Not if it would be "followed by a system of government modeled on the corrupt system of English Government." And here Paine made a most important move: He offered a vivid picture of what the Americans were against—now he would give them something to be for—a republic.

Paine then laid out his own plan for a truly representative system of government. He called for the creation of a national legislature and state assemblies based on broad suffrage. Popular representation would be assured by frequent elections. And a written constitution would guarantee the rights of persons and property and establish freedom of religion. In this he was not at all vague or general. It was time for specific proposals, and he supplied them.

He was just as practical in writing the fourth and last part of his pamphlet. Here he wanted to make Americans feel confident that they had the ability to free themselves from colonialism. Do it now, he insisted, for "the present time is preferable to all others." He mustered all the evidence he could find to show that America could sustain the high cost of war. It had the natural resources to defend itself, raise its own fleet, and beat the Royal Navy. America was not weak measured against Britain. The reverse was true. "There is something absurd," he wrote, "in supposing a continent to be perpetually governed by an island."

He finished with a summary of the practical case for a declaration of independence. He punched it home by arguing that such a declaration would bring offers of much-needed help from Britain's old rivals, France and Spain.

What Paine had done in *Common Sense* was to prove that independence was desirable, was necessary, and was possible.

This he did in clear, direct language, "language as plain as the alphabet," he said. He did not screen his argument behind dazzling eloquence. The facts, first of all the facts! Only those can truly inform the mind.

But feelings, too—they were just as important, Paine believed. Feelings, he wrote, "distinguished us from the herd of common animals. The social compact would dissolve, and justice be extirpated from the earth, or have only a casual existence were we callous to the touches of affection."

Many years later he wrote to a friend that "Some people can be reasoned into sense, and others must be shocked into it. Say a bold thing that will stagger them, and they will begin to think."

He wanted to balance reason and feeling. Yet he did it not without anger, for that tone is evident in *Common Sense*. It came out of Paine's experience in England. All the sorrows, the trials, the humiliations, the injustice he had lived through reverberated in the pamphlet. When he brought in the Norman invasion of England, to show his contempt for how a line of kings was established, he wrote: "A French bastard landing with an armed banditti and establishing himself king of England against the consent of the natives is in plain terms a very paltry rascally original."

If it were not enough to rouse his readers, he salted it with irreverent humor. "In England," he said, "a king hath little more to do than to make war and give away places; which, in plain terms, is to impoverish the nation and set it together by the ears. A pretty business indeed for a man to be allowed 800,000 sterling a year for, and worshipped into the bargain! Of more worth is one honest man to society, and in the sight of God, than all the crowned ruffians that ever lived."

The anger erupted again and again, as when Paine wrote that "no man was a warmer wisher for reconciliation than myself" before the battle of Lexington and Concord. But when he heard the news he "rejected the hardened, sullen-tempered Pharaoh of England forever; and disdain the wretch, that with the pretended title of Father of His People can unfeelingly hear of their slaughter, and composedly sleep with their blood upon his soul."

If he was full of anger with the British government he was just as full of hope for America. His adopted country, he said, held the key to the future of humankind. The cause of America is in a great measure the cause of all mankind. Once independent, America would be the sanctuary for the persecuted people of Europe. From the events to come in America's struggle for freedom, millions everywhere would one day receive their own freedom. Freedom the world over, he was certain, depended upon the fate of America.

As he finished *Common Sense,* Paine offered in beautiful language a moving vision of what American independence would mean:

We have it in our power to begin the world over again... the birthday of a new world is at hand. O ye that love mankind! Ye that dare oppose not only tyranny but the tyrant, stand forth! Every spot of the old world is overrun with oppression. Freedom hath been hunted round the globe. Asia and Africa have long expelled her. Europe regards her as a stranger and England hath given her warning to depart. O! receive the fugitive, and prepare in time an asylum for mankind.

❖ 9 ❖

AN ASTOUNDING

SUCCESS

Who would have predicted the astounding effect of *Common Sense*? Not even the largest-circulation newspapers of the colonies ran to more than two thousand a week. Most pamphlets reached only a few thousand readers. But the demand for Paine's pamphlet rushed it through twenty-five editions in a single year. Many newspapers from New Hampshire to Georgia reprinted its most biting paragraphs. Hundreds of thousands of readers devoured *Common Sense*; many others who could not read had it read aloud to them.

Paine put into print their deepest concerns. "We were blind," said one reader, "but on reading these enlightening words the scales have fallen from our eyes."

No one before Paine had appealed to the common man, to the artisans, farmers, and small shopkeepers who never sat in legislatures. These were the people who had to be convinced and aroused if the war was to be won. As he lowered the standing of kings, Paine raised his readers' sense of self-worth and independence. He helped them come of age. George Washington said that "the sound doctrine and unanswerable reasoning contained in the pamphlet *Common Sense* will not leave members [of the Continental Congress] at a loss to decide upon the propriety of separation."

One reader said the pamphlet "struck a string which required but a touch to make it vibrate. The country was ripe for independence, and only needed somebody to tell the people so, with decision, boldness and plausibility." A Virginian noted that "the public sentiment which a few weeks before had shuddered at the tremendous obstacles with which independence was environed, overleaped every barrier." In Massachusetts a citizen said he believed "no pages were ever more eagerly read, nor more generally approved. People speak of it in rapturous praise."

A British historian, George Trevelyan, writing a history of the American Revolution long after, commented on the impact of the pamphlet, which by February 1776 everyone knew was written by Tom Paine:

> *It would be difficult to name any human composition which has had an effect at once so instant, so extended and so lasting.... It was pirated, parodied and imitated, and translated into the language of every country where the new republic had well-wishers. It worked nothing short of miracles.*

It was not that Paine expressed new or original ideas. His brilliant gift was to combine those ideas into one powerful argument that linked them to the everyday experience of Americans. And he went beyond that to forecast a utopian society that a newly freed people would build.

The huge sales of the pamphlet could have put much-needed money into Paine's pockets. But he was not the kind of man out to get rich quick. He contributed the profits of *Common Sense* to the war effort. The money paid for gloves needed by Washington's troops. Later Paine wrote, "I defend the cause of the poor...but above all, I defend the cause of humanity." He always tried to live by a commitment to the public good, and was consequently rarely well off.

Popular politics was galvanized by the intense discussion the pamphlet aroused. Many challenged the authority of respected leaders, old ideas were scrapped or reshaped, and new ones created. The press overflowed with the pros and cons of independence. As wide agreement was reached on the need for a republican government, it became clear that many differed on how best to structure it.

The Loyalists, supporters of the king, defended the British constitution and reviled Paine as "a crack-brained zealot for democracy" and a "violent republican." How could "every silly clown and illiterate mechanic" design a government! Wouldn't the result be chaos and violence, or even dictatorship?

But others, while they agreed on the need for independence, didn't like Paine's ideas on a new government. John Adams of Massachusetts was their foremost spokesman. He challenged Paine's proposals as too "democratical." Adams wrote his own pamphlet, *Thoughts on Government*, to spread his ideas.

Paine believed that man's natural goodness would create a free society, that is, if he were freed from the chains of corrupt institutions. Adams, however, didn't think men were innately trustworthy. That was why America needed a political system that would restrain and control them.

What bothered Adams especially was the leveling spirit of *Common Sense*: the notion that everyone was as good as everyone else and that everyone should have a hand in shaping the country's destiny. Paine believed in full equality, that there should be only one house in the republic's legislature, which would express the will of the people. Adams was realistic about class distinctions in America; they inevitably meant class conflict. He believed that self-interest drove people's actions and that you had to provide ways to check as well as represent the people. His proposals would give the wealthy class control of an upper house, to provide a check upon actions of the lower house where the commoners sat.

Paine took Adams's criticism in bad temper. When the Adams pamphlet appeared Paine rushed over to Adams's boarding house in Philadelphia to protest the publication, calling it "repugnant." He refused to see that a majority of voters or their representatives could abuse their power and, therefore, needed some restraint—a bicameral legislature, an independent judiciary, a veto-wielding executive. But Adams realized even revolutionaries can make mistakes. Who doesn't? He thought Paine's ill-tempered response to criticism was evidence of his great conceit, a trait that made enemies.

By May 1776 the Continental Congress was using the term states and not colonies, and was advising the states to establish governments independent of Britain. On June 7 a

Jefferson discusses his draft of the Declaration of Independence, influenced by Paine's ideas, with the committee assigned to draw it up.

Virginia delegate introduced an independence resolution in the Continental Congress. The delegates debated the resolution for several days, meanwhile appointing a committee to draft a declaration of independence, just in case. On July 2, the congress resolved that these United Colonies are, and of right ought to be, free and independent states. Thomas Jefferson, then only thirty-three, drafted the Declaration of Independence, with the help of Benjamin Franklin and John Adams.

Paine had met Jefferson in Philadelphia, when the young lawyer arrived for the Continental Congress. He would become a close friend, and their relationship would continue for the rest of Paine's life.

The job that Paine had begun with *Common Sense* was finished by Jefferson. So far as we know, Paine had no direct hand in drafting the Declaration. But Paine's ideas influenced the debate, and his reasoning, in the end, prevailed. Everyone had read his pamphlet, and he visited congressmen to urge them to vote yes.

On July 4 the Declaration of Independence was adopted. Its aim, Jefferson wrote later, was not to say something new. Rather, it was "to place before mankind the common sense of the subject, in terms so plain and firm as to command their assent.... It was intended to be an expression of the American mind." A mind powerfully shaped by Paine's writing.

The Declaration aimed at no social revolution. The great phrase, "all men are created equal," would be interpreted in a limited way. Men like Paine took the promise of "life, liberty and the pursuit of happiness" to mean considerably more than the colonial elite meant by it. For example, Paine tried to have an antislavery clause inserted into the Declaration, but it was withdrawn after objections from the slaveholding delegates from Georgia and South Carolina, as well as from northern suppliers of slaves.

Ideas about republican government shaped the constitutions the states began to write in 1776. Right after July 4 radical democracy triumphed in Pennsylvania when the state adopted a constitution that discharged the notion of checks and balances. A convention presided over by Benjamin Franklin created a unicameral legislature, elected annually, with no property qualifications required either of the legislators or of the voters. The influence of Paine, though he was not present, was especially plain in the debate. And way back then, more than two hundred years ago, the popular desire for term limits guaranteed that the state legislators could not serve for more than four terms. Pennsylvania's old elite gave way to new men representing new constituencies. It was the most advanced state constitution adopted during the American Revolution. But half the people seemed to be against it, and after a short and stormy reign, a totally new constitution was enacted in 1790.

Meanwhile, Tom Paine had gone from civilian to soldier.

❖ 10 ❖
"THESE ARE THE TIMES THAT TRY MEN'S SOULS"

A few days after the Declaration of Independence was adopted, Paine volunteered for the Continental army. He went to Perth Amboy, New Jersey, to serve in a military unit, much like guerrilla fighters, whose job was to rush their help to trouble spots. In August a British fleet landed thirty thousand troops at the present-day site of Brooklyn, New York, and the Battle of Long Island began.

General Washington, with a miserable ragtag army, was up against great odds. The men served for only a year, earned seven dollars a month, had to buy their own uniforms, and were poorly armed. Often they were without gloves, food, and ammunition. Ill trained, if trained at all, they were an undisciplined crowd, not much of a threat to Britain's own crack troops and the Hessian mercenaries King George had hired. If Washington had not staged a masterly retreat on the night of August 29, the war might have ended then and there.

The thirteen separate states were not yet bound into a nation. Paine seems to have been the first to use the name "The United States of America," but as yet it was more an idea than a reality. Both the states and their militias acted like independent powers. Paine saw what giant steps must be taken if the bold words of *Common Sense* and of the

Declaration of Independence were to bear fruit in true independence.

Late in September, Paine was reassigned as aide-de-camp to General Nathaniel Greene, who commanded the troops at Fort Lee and Fort Washington, opposite one another on the banks of the Hudson River. Greene's orders were to prevent the British from taking the Hudson Valley, which would cut off New England from the rest of the states. For two months, from Fort Lee, Paine was able to observe the moves of both sides in the war. He became the field correspondent for the Philadelphia press, writing eyewitness reports of the fighting. His dispatches were sharp and detailed, making the readers feel they, too, were on the scene. He did his best to raise the crumbling morale of the Americans, even though he had little positive to report.

Then came a terrible loss. On November 6 the British surrounded Fort Washington and captured the garrison of two thousand men and all their equipment. In a sudden surprise move the British attacked Fort Lee, too, making Greene's troops flee "like scared rabbits," a Britisher reported gleefully.

As the Continentals retreated through New Jersey, Paine reported the rout for the *Pennsylvania Journal*. While he did not hide the awful facts, and got across the great danger of the moment, he managed to avoid intensifying the panic that the already frightened citizenry felt.

The British followed the Americans over to the New Jersey shore and then on up to the Delaware River. With his forces so weak, Washington had no choice but to retreat and retreat or risk losing his army. It had shrunk to three thousand men. Soldiers who had completed their short term packed up and went home. Many others deserted, and the fresh militia the general expected did not turn up.

Retreating with the troops, Paine saw how demoralized they were. What if the British now tried to take Philadelphia, the capital city? What could prevent it? Paine heard that the congress had fled for safety to Baltimore, that the printing presses had quit publishing, and that no one knew what was happening. With the consent of his superior officers, he left Trenton and walked the thirty miles to Philadelphia, risking capture by the enemy.

When he reached the city he found refugees fleeing, and Tories preparing to give the British army a royal welcome. The citizens, Paine reported, were in a "deplorable and melancholy condition...afraid to speak and almost to think... and nothing in circulation but fears and falsehoods."

If the British captured Philadelphia, the Revolution would be in danger. Paine felt he had to do something to pull the Americans up out of the depths of despair. In a "passion of patriotism," as he said later, "I wrote the first number of the Crisis. It was published on the 19th of December, which was the very blackest of times."

Throughout the long years of the war, an agonizing time of many losses and few victories, Paine would try to keep up the morale of the Americans with essays on the progress and meaning of the war. From 1776 to the final victory at Yorktown in 1783 he wrote eighteen pieces, calling them *The American Crisis*, and signing each one "Common Sense." They thrill with the superb phrases so typical of his writing.

On Christmas Eve, General Washington ordered the Crisis to be read aloud to the troops as they prepared for the battle of Trenton. It opened with these lines that would become as memorable as the Gettysburg Address:

> *These are the times that try men's souls.*
> *The summer soldier and the sunshine*
> *patriot will, in this crisis, shrink from the*
> *service of their country; but he that stands*
> *it now, deserves the love and thanks of*
> *man and woman. Tyranny, like hell, is not*
> *easily conquered; yet we have this consola-*
> *tion with us, that the harder the conflict,*
> *the more glorious the triumph. What we*
> *obtain too cheap, we esteem too lightly: it*
> *is dearness only that gives every thing its*
> *value. Heaven knows how to put a proper*

*price upon its goods; and it would be
strange indeed if so celestial an article as
freedom should not be highly rated.
Britain, with an army to enforce her
tyranny, has declared that she has a right
(not only to TAX) but "TO BIND US IN
ALL CASES WHATSOEVER," and if
being bound in that manner, is not slavery, then is there not such a thing as slavery upon the earth...*

One day later, on Christmas night, 1776, Washington
struck at the British, crossing the Delaware River into New
Jersey. He surprised the Hessian troops celebrating the holiday in Trenton. It was "a glorious victory," reported one of
Washington's young aides. "It will rejoice the hearts of our
friends everywhere and give new life to our hitherto wan-
ing fortunes."

Many agree that Paine's rousing pamphlet helped
Washington carry the day. (Paine's biographer John Keane
calls it "among the greatest political essays in the modern
English language.") That first *Crisis* paper, like many others to come, was picked up and published in newspapers
throughout the country. With perfect timing, Paine took up
issue after issue as they arose, concentrating on the hard
problems confronting the nation struggling to survive.

He never relented on King George, calling him "a sot-
tish, stupid, stubborn, worthless, brutish man." As for
George's American loyalists, they were nothing but "cowards, serving the king out of slavish, self-interested fear."
Paine drove home to his readers the crucial choice: either
continue to fight for victory on the battlefield or suffer the
terrible fate of a "ravaged country" and "slavery without
hope."

In January 1777 Paine was asked to serve as secretary
to a commission negotiating on behalf of the Pennsylvania
Assembly and the Continental Congress with tribes of the
Iroquois living in the region.

The Indians were concerned with their status under

the new republic government. The four-day session met in Easton, fifty miles north of Philadelphia. Paine had some experience with Native Americans. He had published a long essay by William Penn on the Indians, and he had talked often with them during his work in Philadelphia, trying to learn their language and understand their culture.

In Easton he was impressed by the physical beauty, the intelligence, and the political skills of the Iroquois delegates. The talks led to a peace treaty, but the Continental Congress soon canceled it. Members disliked the way the Indians—to protect their lands and culture—played off one group of whites against another. Only a minority of Native Americans supported the American Revolution, which infuriated many white leaders. They called the Indians "beasts of prey" and "bloodhounds." The Declaration of Independence referred to them as "merciless savages."

One English traveler in America at this time noted that "white Americans have the most rancorous antipathy to the whole race of Indians." "Nothing," he said, "is more common than to hear them talk of extirpating them from the face of the earth—men, women and children."

But Paine was no racist. He spoke of the Native Americans as his "brothers" and praised their love of liberty and their refusal to give up their independence. Their sense of equality, too, impressed him. Later he wrote that among them "there is not...any of those spectacles of human misery which poverty and want present to our eyes in all the towns and cities in Europe.... The life of an Indian is a continual holiday, compared with the poor of Europe."

A victory over the British at Princeton led a more hopeful congress to return to Philadelphia in March 1777. It set about constructing a foreign policy meant to win foreign allies for the war against Britain. In April, Paine, just turned forty, was appointed secretary to the new Committee on Foreign Affairs. Only one congressman opposed him, charging Paine with being "a very intemperate, bad character." (Gossip about hard drinking would follow Paine the rest of his days.)

This appointment, the first official recognition of his

achievements, delighted Paine. It went a bit to his head, for he was heard to brag that he was "Secretary of Foreign Affairs." But his duties were really to keep the committee records and draft its correspondence to agents abroad, such as Franklin in Paris. He needed the modest pay and enjoyed being in on important and secret matters.

Early that autumn the British began to move on Philadelphia. Washington marched out to meet the enemy at Brandywine Creek, but once again the Continentals were badly beaten. By evening Paine heard the news of the rout. To forestall panic in the capital he worked all night on a *Crisis* pamphlet and rushed it to the printer in the morning. Don't despair, he told his readers. We have the advantage of a citizens' army operating on our home soil and can double and redouble our numbers. But the British are cut off from all supplies and "must sooner or later inevitably fall into our hands."

The terrified Philadelphians were not reassured. A third of the city's population fled, while the state government ran off to Lancaster and the congress to York. The British took over the capital, and Paine, a man marked for execution, left in a hurry. For the next nine months he was a sort of roving reporter, doing all he could to obtain accurate news and send it to Pennsylvania's officials as well as to the congress.

There was little good news to report. Near victory at a battle in Germantown, a suburb of Philadelphia, the Americans suddenly panicked and suffered casualties twice the number of the British.

Better news arrived from the North. A British army under General John Burgoyne had been trying to split the colonies by gaining control of New York. After some minor bouts he fought the main match with the Americans at Saratoga and lost heavily. On October 17, 1777, Burgoyne was forced to surrender his entire army of about five thousand.

It was the kind of glorious victory for the Americans that Paine had long promised his readers; it was a disaster for the British. Burgoyne's defeat convinced the European enemies of Britain that this was the time to settle old scores. A few months later France signed a treaty with the United States promising to assist it in the war. Spain, and Holland too, soon came in on the side of the Americans.

Louis XVI saw Saratoga as a critical turning point in the war. He placed France on America's side not because he loved liberty but because he hoped to weaken Britain and gain back some of the empire France had lost, especially Canada. French liberals like the young Marquis de Lafayette were eager to join America in its fight against tyranny.

When the great news came of the victory at Saratoga, General Washington, with his main army near Philadelphia, was preparing for the winter. The cold months and the deep snows killed any thought of fighting. For winter quarters, Washington chose Valley Forge, a crossroads twenty miles from Philadelphia. It was "the winter of despair" for his eleven thousand troops. They were des-

At General Washington's winter quarters at Valley Forge, Paine witnessed the terrible suffering of the American troops.

perately short of blankets, shoes, clothing, and food. On December 18, 1777, the tired and hungry men pitched their tents and began to cut down trees to make log cabins.

That winter Paine wrote letters to Franklin, who was drumming up French aid in Paris. Paine gave him an optimistic picture of American prospects: "We rub and drive on, beyond whatever could be expected, and instead of wondering why some things have not been done better, the greater wonder is we have done so well."

So well? Paine had made himself believe a happy ending to the war was inevitable, and it colored his reports. But the truth was, as he walked with General Washington along the soldiers' huts he saw how many were half-frozen, infected with disease, dying of starvation. While nearby in Philadelphia the British and the Tories who had welcomed them were enjoying luxurious living.

Late in January, Paine walked the 120 miles to York to resume duties with the Committee on Foreign Affairs. But there was nothing for him to do, and he quit the village for Lancaster. There he wrote another *Crisis* paper, urging readers to maintain their solidarity and continue the fight. He said nothing about the suffering at Valley Forge nor an aborted attempt by some in congress to sack Washington for military incompetency and replace him with General Horatio Gates, the victor at Saratoga. If Paine had told all he knew, he would only have deepened demoralization. He opted for secrecy, believing military success demanded it. It must have been hard to do, for he was one who believed in freedom of information and debate if citizens were to achieve a democratic republic.

It troubled him then, and the same dilemma would occur many more times. How could citizens protect themselves against arbitrary power if they were denied the truth?

❖ 11 ❖

ANOTHER WAR—
AGAINST GREED

In December 1778, Paine became embroiled in a bitter public issue: war profiteering. That men would place self-interest above public virtue appalled Paine. He had seen greed operating freely in England at every level of business and government. Here in this new land he had hoped to see a democratic commonwealth created that would be guided by public-spirited citizens. Yet some of the leading revolutionaries were openly declaring that you could never expect people to set aside their personal wants and aspirations for the sake of the public good.

One example was the wealthy Philadelphia merchant and congressman Robert Morris, who had elevated private greed to a principle. "It is inconsistent with the principles of liberty," he said, "to prevent a man from the free disposal of his property on such terms as he may think fit." In other words, anything goes, if it will put money in your pocket.

Now the spotlight focused on what was called the Silas Deane affair. It went back to 1776, when the French, Britain's enemy during the recent Seven Years' War, tried to help the Americans by secretly supplying military clothing, cannon, muskets, and ammunition for the Continental army.

A dummy company had been set up to handle the secret transfer of war materials. Its prime agents were Beaumarchais, the French playwright and friend of Louis XVI, and Silas Deane, a wealthy congressman from

Connecticut sent abroad to handle the American side of the negotiations. Deane was to have all his expenses covered, plus a five percent commission on the value of what the French supplied. It was not clear whether the supplies were to be gifts or would be sold to the Americans at a reasonable price.

The French and the Spanish governments, plus French financiers, funded the deal with three million livres in gold. The French supplies arrived in a dozen ships over the next year. But some Americans privy to the secret negotiations smelled corruption. They believed Beaumarchais and probably Deane too had profiteered outrageously by billing at five times the actual costs.

As secretary of the Foreign Affairs Committee, Paine had seen documents that confirmed the charges against Deane. When Deane returned home he claimed innocence during secret committee hearings. (Much later, evidence came to light that proved Deane had not only dealt corruptly with French aid but, for handsome pay, had conspired with the British government against the American Revolution.)

The committee doubted his innocence, and Deane took his case to the public through the medium of the press. His denial of guilt angered Paine, who was already deeply disturbed by several recent corruption scandals involving government officials. And now here was Silas Deane grabbing illicit profits from wartime contracts while the soldiers at Valley Forge suffered unbearably.

It disgusted General Washington too, who lamented that "an insatiable thirst for riches seems to have got the better of every other consideration and almost of every order of men."

To bring down Deane, Paine revealed in several newspaper articles secret information about French aid that had come across his committee desk. It was a move that would cause Paine great trouble. The disclosures embarrassed France, and the French minister to America protested to the congress, insisting that Paine be punished. The result was a congressional hearing that gave Paine little chance to pre-

Silas Deane, the lawyer and diplomat embroiled with Paine in a controversy over charges of corruption.

sent his case. He was sharply criticized, both by those who feared his actions endangered the desired alliance with France and by others who detested Paine for his radical views. One of these was a powerful congressman, Gouverneur Morris. A conservative and a snob, he attacked Paine as a "mere adventurer from England, without fortune, without family or connections, ignorant even of grammar."

Another wealthy Morris, Robert (no relation), joined in the attack. Paine's articles had accused this Morris of misusing his power as the government's purchaser of military supplies to steer hugely profitable contracts to his own company as well as to friends, among them Deane. Were such shabby dealings in the public interest, Paine asked? He called for a public investigation.

Heavy counterattacks, including charges that Paine was a traitor to the Revolution, did not make him back down. Free speech, he insisted, included the right to print truths that powerful people didn't want to hear.

Luckily the Deane affair did not prevent France and America from signing the Treaty of Alliance in 1788. But the claim that Paine had violated the secrecy to which his job committed him cost him heavily. He was forced to resign. But he would not go quietly. In a letter to the congress he denied any wrongdoing and said, "I have betrayed no trust because I have constantly employed that trust to the public good. I have revealed no secrets because I have told nothing that was, or I conceive ought to be a secret. I have convicted Mr. Deane of error, and in so doing I hope that I have done my duty."

The Deane affair hurt Paine so badly that months later he confessed to George Washington that he had had "a most exceeding rough time.... I fell, all at once, from high credit to disgrace, and the worst word was thought too good for me."

Men continued to humiliate him with insults on the floor of the Congress, denouncing him as an enemy of the common cause. He was even beaten on the streets of Philadelphia and vilified in the press through anonymous articles and letters. Determined to hit back, Paine's friends organized a public rally in his support. Standing in the State House yard, several thousand people yelled "Yes!" to a resolution "that Mr. Thomas Paine is considered by this meeting as a friend to the American cause, and therefore... we will support and defend him, so long as his conduct shall continue to prove him to be a friend to this country."

Out of a job, Paine feared sinking back into poverty once again. A chance to escape it came right after he resigned, when a French emissary offered him a large salary of one thousand dollars a year to write articles on behalf of the Franco-American alliance against the British. Paine refused the offer, considering it a bribe. He would not violate his principles as a political writer. To take the money for voicing the views of a political party or a government was wrong, he believed. He was not a hack writer, selling himself to pen whatever a client asked.

He would have gone in a hurry if he had not accepted

the only other job offered him. Owen Biddle, a prominent Quaker merchant, and a sympathizer, hired him as an office clerk. Menial work, it paid barely enough for board and room, a bit of snuff, and now and then a shot of brandy or rum.

The price of everything he needed to live on had gone sky-high. Inflation was making the dollar almost worthless. What was to blame? The merchants' high prices were the effect, not the cause of inflation. And they opposed any talk of having the government control prices.

To Paine this was deceptive reasoning. The merchants were trying to conceal their selfish interests. He had already argued in print that living, breathing labor, not property, is the basic source of material wealth. "Where there are none to labor, and but few to consume, land and property is not riches," he said. Can property alone "defend a country against invading enemies? House and lands cannot fight; sheep and oxen cannot be taught the musket; therefore the defence must be personal, and that which equally unites all must be something equally the property of all, viz. an equal share of freedom, independent of the varieties of wealth."

In England, Paine had observed how the propertied rich used the laws to further enrich themselves and to exploit the poor. He did not want this to happen in this new nation. Men of property should not be allowed to trample on common humanity. He would write about this time and again.

The problem of rising inflation was uppermost in people's minds that spring of 1779. Paine's view that prices should be regulated by government was widely known. The Continental Congress had refused to do it, holding it was the problem of the states. Popular support placed Paine on several committees to investigate inflation. But when their reports advocated various schemes to check inflation, most merchants, and artisans, too, vigorously opposed them. They feared popular control of economic decisions. Business should be left to businessmen, not to the ignorant mass. So inflation continued to run wild. Paine noted that he had to pay three hundred paper dollars for one pair of worsted stockings.

Late that summer Paine was felled again by a fever, as bad as the illness that had almost killed him on the voyage to America. For many weeks he lay helpless in his rented room. Friends came to look after him. The physical and emotional battering of the past year weakened and depressed him. To his friend Henry Laurens he wrote: "I know but one kind of life I am fit for, and that is a thinking one, and, of course, a writing one—but I have confined myself so much of late, taken so little exercise, and lived so very sparingly, that unless I alter my way of life it will alter me."

His job had ended while he was confined to bed. Needing work, he appealed to the Pennsylvania state government for help. The assembly, controlled now by the Radicals, voted to appoint Paine its clerk. It was a happy turn for him. His spirits lifted. He had a salary, and he again plunged into politics. Some of his chores were routine and boring. But his job was more important than its title sounds. As the close friend and adviser of assembly leaders, he was able to influence the program of reform the newly elected Radical majority stood for.

A top priority for Paine and many delegates was to get rid of slavery. The Radicals had long opposed both the slave trade and the institution of slavery. Slavery existed everywhere in the thirteen states, both north and south. Every one of them protected the institution in its laws. By now nearly one of every five people were enslaved. In Pennsylvania itself there were six thousand slaves.

The Declaration of Independence had proudly asserted the natural rights of man, but it made no mention of slavery. How could people fighting for liberty hold blacks in bondage? As an anonymous writer in the *Pennsylvania Chronicle* put it, "How suits it with the glorious cause of Liberty, to keep your fellow men in bondage, men equally the work of your great creator, men formed for freedom as yourselves?"

A typical broadside, advertising the auction of Africans just arrived on a slave ship, incited Paine to campaign against the slave trade and slavery.

Moral challenges such as this and military expediency broke down barriers and led most states to enlist slaves and free blacks. During the war years black soldiers would fight in virtually every major military action. In return for their military service most states freed slaves upon enlistment or at the end of service.

In Pennsylvania, early and persistent Quaker opposition to slavery advanced the cause of emancipation. In 1775, only a few weeks after Paine published his essay against the African slave trade—and partly inspired by it—the first abolition society in the world was formed in Philadelphia. Its member believed African-Americans were unlawfully held in bondage. They set out to pressure the

Pennsylvania Assembly to outlaw slavery. Resistance came from slaveholders and merchants who profited by the forced labor of black men, women, and children. They did not like a bill that would interfere with slavery. To get a law passed its backers had to compromise with the opposition. The bill finally agreed upon was adopted on March 1, 1780. Many historians believe that Paine wrote the preamble to the law.

But the law did not free anyone then in slavery. It did, however, provide that children born to slaves from then on could no longer be held in bondage for life. They had to be freed at the age of twenty-eight. Abusive treatment of slaves by masters was forbidden.

The final outcome disappointed abolitionists and of course, the slaves. To wait for freedom for twenty-eight years! And at a time when the average age of death for slaves was less than that! Nor did the law set a final date when slavery would be totally abolished. Still, for Paine and many others the new law was a signal to the world that the evil of American slavery was on its way to being ended.

If the antislavery law gave Paine some satisfaction, nothing else at the moment did. The news of the war continued to be bad. Reports came in that the troops were half starved, half naked, and that some officers had given up all hope. Paine warned that "a hungry man will soon be a seditious one." On May 12, Charleston, South Carolina, surrendered after heavy bombardment by the British, who took thousands prisoner and captured great stores of weapons and ammunition.

Paine urged upon the state leaders a new plan to draft men and to place heavier taxes upon the rich to pay for an expanded army. He himself donated five hundred pounds saved from his pay and pledged another like sum. The desperate situation moved the merchants to create the first bank in the country, the Bank of Pennsylvania, with wealthy men subscribing large sums to supply the army with wages, arms, and equipment. Declaring Paine was already poor enough, the bankers returned his contribution.

He wrote another pamphlet in the *Crisis* series to show the British that the loss of Charleston had not broken the American will to fight on. His old excitement returned as he poured renewed energy into writing. His patriotic labors were recognized by the University of Pennsylvania, which awarded him an honorary master of arts degree that Fourth of July.

Later in the year Paine decided to do something about the need to build unity among the states. Conflicts of interest and regional rivalries were crippling cooperation during the war. Back in 1777, the congress had adopted the Articles of Confederation, providing for a permanent frame of government to bind the states together. But ratification by the states had been delayed by quarrels over land claims. Paine proposed that a national convention be held to write a constitution that would create a stronger central authority to coordinate interests and ensure order. His pamphlet, *Public Good*, appeared on December 30, 1780. The first to make this appeal, he was anticipating the Constitutional Convention that would be held seven years later. It did not go down well with some of his radical republican friends. They feared a strong central government would become a tyrannical power.

Perhaps weary of such clashes, he began to talk about returning to England. The radicalism of the Wilkes movement Paine had been part of at home gathered momentum. Elected to Parliament the year Paine left for America, John Wilkes had championed the liberties of the American colonies and fought for parliamentary reform. He defended freedom of the press and the rights of the electorate. Wasn't it time for Paine to join that fight? Why couldn't the people make a republican revolution in England as they were doing in America? With all his experience in America he would be able to help his countrymen see the possibilities open to them.

But Paine's friends thought the plan was "both difficult and dangerous." He would not listen to their objections. He resigned his committee post and was about to sail for England when Major John André, a British spy, was captured and swiftly tried and executed. The news frightened Paine; he realized he would suffer the same fate if the British government got its hands on him.

He dropped his plan, only to find, a week later, another way to go abroad. The congress was sending an American mission to seek more financial aid from France. Although Franklin was already in Paris to advocate the American cause, the congress felt fresh support was needed. Paine volunteered to help. He would pay his own way out of his savings and join two young emissaries, John Laurens and William Jackson, as their private companion and adviser.

On February 11, 1781, they sailed from Boston on the *Alliance*, bound for France.

❖ 12 ❖

A Pen for Hire?

It was a rough voyage.

On the fifth night out, the *Alliance*, sailing in the North Atlantic, ran into huge drifting icebergs. The captain feared the ship would break apart if it collided with the mountains of ice towering overhead. Near midnight an ice floe crashed into the wooden ship and gashed a big hole in the port side. For seven hours the ship heaved about in the terrifying dark, the wind moaning and howling and ripping one of the mainsails in two.

Paine was sweating in panic, doubting the ship would survive. But just before daybreak the fury eased off, and the passengers thanked God they had come through. As the crew made repairs, the *Alliance* encountered a "glorious breeze" that "carried us from nine to twelve miles an hour for seven days," Paine said. After a month at sea they reached the French coast and docked at L'Orient on March 9, 1781. Local officials and citizens greeted them warmly and paid Paine "great compliments" on his internationally known publications.

Before setting off for Paris, Paine visited Nantes, about a hundred miles away. There a Philadelphian named Elkanah Watson spent some time with Paine, introducing him around and acting as his interpreter. (Paine never learned to speak French well.) At an official reception for him, Paine made a strange impression. Although everyone admired him for his writings, this odd-looking man shocked them. He clothes were filthy, he smelled bad, and he kept scratching himself all over—an itch he had contracted aboard ship.

Watson recalled, many years later, that Paine was "coarse and uncouth in his manners, loathsome in his appearance, and a disgusting egotist; rejoicing most in talking of himself, and reading the effusions of his own mind." Watson plunged him into a hot tub and kept him soaking and scrubbing there for an hour, until the "brimstone odor" disappeared, and then loaned Paine a clean shirt.

Moving on to Paris, Paine stayed with Laurens and Jackson at Franklin's home in Passy, on the city's outskirts. Franklin's diplomatic skills (he was now seventy-five) and the vivid firsthand accounts of the revolution's critical condition brought by the three eyewitnesses helped convince the French to make a grant of six million livres and loans worth another ten million.

Paine's role was to organize the military and economic data needed for the negotiations and to write the reports, memoranda, and letters to the Foreign Ministry that documented the gravity of the situation. Some two months after they arrived in France, the Americans happily watched a French ship sail off to America, with the Marquis de Lafayette aboard, carrying clothing for twenty thousand troops and arms and ammunition. Much more was to come. The French promised they would send a great fleet to America that summer to give direct fighting support.

The success of the mission delighted Paine. But what would he do next? Should be stay in Europe? Should he go back to America? He told young Laurens of his grave doubts: "Though I had every wish it was possible for a man to feel for the success of the cause which America was engaged in, yet such had been the treatment I had experienced year after year, that I had not heart to return back and was resolved not to do it."

He changed his mind; why, we don't know. On June 1, he and Laurens boarded a heavily armed French frigate bound for America. Because the ship carried millions in silver for American aid, it sailed in convoy with other warships. It was painfully slow going as the convoy maneuvered endlessly to avoid enemy action. On August 26, after eighty-six days at sea, Paine finally landed in Boston.

The generous gift from France came too late to be of much value. But the French deserved the deepest gratitude for great aid provided earlier. In July 1780 they had sent over General Rochambeau with five thousand regulars, and then a powerful naval force under Admiral de Grasse. Coordinated French and American action penned up the British commander, Lord Cornwallis, on the York peninsula. And on October 19, 1781, he was forced to give up at Yorktown, surrendering his entire army of seven thousand men. With the latest French gift not needed for the war, the congress ordered the cash to be handed to Robert Morris, the new superintendent of finance. He used the money as capital stock for converting the Bank of Pennsylvania into the Bank of North America.

Such a conclusion to the French mission was an anticlimax for Paine. No one paid any attention to the role he had played. Who even noticed that he had returned to Philadelphia? His pride was hurt, and he began to feel sorry for himself. It depressed him all the more to find that the conservatives had taken political leadership while he was gone. The Articles of Confederation had been ratified by the states, and the first congress under the new establishment had met. His chief supporters, the Radicals, had receded into the background.

Here he was, stranded, a freelance journalist, and like any other, uncertain where his next dollar would come from. No matter how great his service to America, it left him with nothing. He carried little weight with the new government and could expect no place in it.

Yet wasn't this just what he had always conceived his role to be? Not a tool of a party, not a mouthpiece for any man. But a free-spirited, independent thinker whose great skill with words made it possible for him to present ideas that made citizens ask questions, challenge authority, check the abuses of power. He was in no mood to view himself objectively, but we, from this distance, can see his great contribution as one of the very first modern political writers.

When the glorious news of the surrender at Yorktown

A wild celebration begins as news of the British surrender at Yorktown reaches the people of Philadelphia.

reached Philadelphia, a frenzied celebration exploded. As express riders galloped from state to state with the news, illuminations, bonfires, rockets, roasted oxen, and overflowing liquor marked the festivities. It was not the end of the war, for sporadic fighting would last another year or so. But in reality the revolution had been won.

Yet here was Paine, jobless and broke. "I now felt myself worse off than ever," he said. His appeals for work were ignored by government officials. Late in November he wrote to General Washington, who was spending the winter in Philadelphia, to inform him of his sorry situation. He was poor, he said, because he had always given up personal profit by channeling the royalties from his work into public causes. Yet now government officials were cold to him, indifferent to his requests for a position, for a clerkship, anything. He asked Washington to use his authority to help him. If not, he said, despite his deep love for America he would have to leave it and return to Europe.

Paine's appeal was answered. Washington spoke with a friend or two, probably Robert Morris, now a great power in the nation's economic affairs, and with the French minister, la Luzerne. Could they help Paine temporarily by offering him some money or a job, at least until a long-term solution could be worked out or perhaps a grant of land when the war ended?

La Luzerne promptly hired Paine "to write a few articles on the advantage gained by the United States through the Alliance" with France. The deal was kept secret, for obvious reasons on the French side, and no doubt because Paine had broken his pledge to himself not to put out his pen for hire. In the next two years the work earned him about a thousand dollars.

Robert Morris acted more slowly. He had already been meeting with Paine to ask his support in promoting public recognition of the usefulness of taxation to finance public needs, such as support of the army still in the field. Paine came up with some ideas as the two got together socially several times. Morris seemed no longer angry with Paine over his sharp criticism of Morris's and other wealthy men's profiteering. And Paine shared some of Morris's economic beliefs, especially that commerce and economic growth were vital to a healthy nation desiring to be at peace with the world. In addition, Morris confessed that he now realized he had been "totally deceived" by that thoroughly bad man, Silas Deane.

In February 1782 a deal was worked out to put Paine to work. In a written agreement with Washington and Robert Livingston, the secretary of financial affairs, Paine would be hired "to inform the people and rouse them to action." His salary would be eight hundred dollars a year, to be paid out of a secret service fund put up by Robert Morris. The goal was "to urge the legislators of the several states to grant sufficient taxes for the American army to be well-fed and clothed, and paid a decent wage" while it finished the war with Britain.

Help was badly needed to break down the resistance of the states to any increase in taxation. But to achieve that

Robert Morris, financier and statesman, helped support Paine's writing when the war ended.

goal it was vital to lay groundwork for a new federal constitution, armed with the power to levy taxes upon the citizens. On his own, Paine had already proposed this very thing back in December 1780 with *Public Good*. So he told Morris he was "well disposed" to do it. Further, he was assured that he could refuse to write on any topic suggested to him and that he need not accept any criticism of his manuscripts.

All agreed that the arrangement should be kept secret. But it leaked quickly. Maybe Paine himself was the source. He wanted his service to be publicly recognized and to have it known that he could veto requests as proof of his independence. Another reason Paine liked his new job was that it gave him the chance to argue publicly for a two-level federated system of republican government elected by the citizenry.

He got to work at once. In 1782 and 1783 he wrote "Six Letters to the Citizens of Rhode Island," published in the *Providence Gazette*, defending the right of the national government to tax individual states. True, in England he had opposed the burden of taxes levied by an oppressive power on a people who had no say in government. But America was different. This was not a despotic regime taxing its subjects while denying them security and freedom. Were that the case, taxation would really be theft. In a free republic, however, a democratically elected government is accountable to its citizens. The people pay their money to fund the operations of a government they trust.

Paine had always favored the centralization of government. Early on, he saw it as the best way to win the war. And now he tried to make his readers see that it was the precondition of a strong democratic nation. What was called laissez-faire economics made sense to him. A free market went hand in hand with a powerful federal authority to promote commercial and territorial expansion. And that, he said, would benefit the common good.

Paine was one of the rare ones who could look ahead to the distant future and anticipate what might be needed at that time. He predicted new states would be formed as emigrants pushed westward and that these states would seek admission to the union. He had outlined a step-by-step process for admission in *Public Good* that later was embodied in the Constitution. His vision fitted with his present advocacy of a stronger central government.

❖ 13 ❖

BANKS AND BRIDGES

As the revolution moved to its close, Paine felt himself more and more a marginal figure. Yes, he was meeting with such upper-class leaders as Morris and Washington, sometimes entertaining them in his own room, over oysters and bread and cheese, while they discussed plans and enjoyed conversation. Still, he could never forget he was of the poor artisan class, a nobody in the eyes of aristocrats who publicly derided him. He was always the outsider, only tolerated for the contribution he made to the success of their joint enterprise, the Revolution.

He began to think he ought to write a history of the American Revolution. He had been at the heart of this unprecedented grand upheaval; he knew many of its leaders; he had seen much with his own eyes. He knew how inaccurate and how biased people's memories of it would be in the remote future. And how some might even deliberately distort what happened to advance their own interests. But his book would be the fresh, immediate response to the historical event. The project never got beyond the dreaming stage. He was always pressed to do the thing needed now, this very minute.

Then one day in the fall of 1781 Robert Morris loaned him that English translation of the French book, called *The American Revolution*, by Abbé Raynal. Disagreeing with much of it, Paine decided to summarize his own views in the form of a commentary on Raynal's book. In August 1782 his pamphlet, the longest he ever wrote, was published in Philadelphia. Raynal claimed that the Americans had wanted independence only because they disliked paying British taxes. Paine took exception to that and to Raynal's notion that a revolution was nothing more than a natural turn of events, like the cycle of the seasons. Paine argued that the American Revolution had fundamentally altered both people's minds—their view of the power and how it should be exercised—and the structure of government that embodied those views. "We see with other eyes; we hear with other ears; and think with other thoughts, than those we formerly used," he wrote. "We can look back on our own prejudices, as if they had been the prejudices of other people."

Raynal worried that the Franco-American alliance was not natural and was sure to end badly. Yes, said Paine, there is a contradiction. France is a despotic monarchy, a symbol of the Old World, while America is a free republic whose seeds of liberty will carry across oceans to take deep root in other parts of the globe. Trade, he argued, can create "universal civilization."

Paine was among the first to see the American Revolution as important not just to Americans but to the whole world. It was a beacon lighting up the way to world citizenship and world peace. Optimistically, Paine wrote that in a new world society, all peoples, of whatever nation, would be seen as "the work of one Creator."

Only ignorance and prejudice, he said, could slow the civilizing process. Then, anticipating what would not happen for generations, the formation of the United Nations, he wrote that commerce and free trade, acting around the world would eventually overcome barriers and bind nations together as never before. And so too would science and literature have a similar peaceful and unifying effect.

These were not new ideas but expressions of the Enlightenment shared by many thinkers. But Paine's way of expressing them reached far beyond Philadelphia. New and cheaper editions of his *Letter to the Abbé Raynal* quickly appeared, with men like Washington and Morris taking quantities to distribute at home and abroad. Copies were soon published in London and Dublin, and five different

French versions appeared in Paris. So impressed was Paine's old patron, la Luzerne, that he sent him a gift of fifty guineas.

On April 18, 1783, General Washington announced that the fighting between Britain and America had ended. The next day Paine published his last *Crisis* paper. "The times that tried men's souls are over," he wrote, "and the greatest and completest revolution the world ever knew, gloriously and happily accomplished."

Now America "has no foreign power to monopolize her commerce, perplex her legislation, or control her prosperity." But he warned that the Revolution had been like "a long and raging hurricane" that did much damage to men's hearts and minds. Now, he went on, America needed to think anew of the community and to seek a rebirth of public spirit. It needed to shape a strong central government, to establish national unity, and to seize the opportunity "to form the noblest, purest constitution on the face of the earth."

It would be four years before the Constitutional Convention would meet in Philadelphia to design the new pattern of government. It would not come about easily. The states had their strong differences, as did the various groups within them: small states against large states, commercial interests against agricultural interests, rich against poor, North against South. It would take intense negotiation and compromise to overcome bitter quarreling and to find common ground on a constitution to govern the new democratic republic.

The revolutionary generation was beginning to see evidence of what a democratic America might mean. If you thought living in a republic meant people would willingly sacrifice their private financial interests for the sake of the common good, were you wrong? Already the marketplace was dominating people's decisions. Americans were not going to be selfless and virtuous, keeping their private interests out of the public arena. George Washington himself had said that to expect ordinary people to be "influenced by any other principles than those of interest, is to

look for what never did, and I fear never will happen....
The few who act upon principles of disinterestedness are,
comparatively speaking, no more than a drop in the
ocean."

With the war's end, Paine's work for Morris and
Washington ended. He had to find other means to earn a
living. In June 1783 he asked the congress to reward him
for his long service to the revolution. He spelled out what
he had done, concluding that while he had "the honor of
being ranked among the founders" of the new nation, he
had no home within it.

Washington supported Paine's plea for help, writing
the congress on his behalf. He suggested that Paine be
appointed official historian of the United States. A congressional committee approved offering Paine the historian's
position, but he refused the offer. He said he was willing to
work for nothing in that capacity, so that as historian he
would be unrestricted in his devotion to the truth. All he
wanted from the congress was compensation for his past
services, not for anything in the future. What he had hoped
for was a grant of government land.

The congress itself never voted on Paine's appeal.
Many members disliked Paine because of bad feelings
roused during the Silas Deane affair. And the congress
itself had no sure source of revenues. Thousands of soldiers
were still unpaid, and what about pensions for them? Even
when congress did act, some of the states simply ignored
its decisions.

Unable to pay his rent, Paine was forced to move out
of his Philadelphia room and move in with friends, the
Kirkbride family, in Bordentown, New Jersey. The summer
of 1783 an epidemic of scarlet fever struck the region and in
October laid Paine low. Feeling better in a month, he was
invited by George Washington to visit him at the country
place congress had given him in Rocky Hill, New Jersey.
For three weeks the two men enjoyed political talk and
tried their hand at a scientific experiment with natural gas.

On one occasion, when they were on their way to
church, Paine's coat was stolen. The general gave him one

of his own coats. Paine would wear it proudly for several years before handing it on to a friend as a special treasure.

Just to be in Washington's company gave Paine great pleasure. When word came that the last British soldiers were leaving New York now that the peace treaty had been signed, Paine rode together with Washington into the city to watch the redcoats sail home. Later that day Paine paraded beside the general in a public demonstration watched by great crowds of citizens celebrating the victory of freedom over tyranny. Then, at Fraunces Tavern on Pearl Street, Paine watched as Washington said his emotional farewell to the officers of his army and left for his home at Mount Vernon.

With his friend gone, Paine tried again to get help. "I am tired of having no home," he wrote to the mayor of New York, "especially in a country where everybody will allow, I have deserved one." Congress had done nothing; maybe one of the states might? It would be good if he could be granted a small piece of the property New York State was now expropriating from Tories who had remained loyal to the king.

Somehow, the facts are not clear, Paine acquired a small house in Bordentown, probably with the money la Luzerne had sent him as a reward for supporting the Franco-American alliance. He moved in at Christmastime. It was the neighborhood he had gotten to know well on his many visits to the Kirkbrides. But dropping in now and then and staying permanently were very different. Quickly he found this was no life for him. The winter was harsh and kept him housebound. Company was scarce, entertainment nonexistent, he didn't know how to run a farm, and he made a mess of cooking and cleaning.

As the winter ended, he learned that the New York legislature had granted him property in New Rochelle, confiscated from a loyalist. It was a farmhouse and three hundred acres, about thirty miles from New York City. With the gift came a handsome tribute: "His literary works... inspired the citizens of this state with unanimity, confirmed their confidence in the rectitude of their cause,

*Paines's cottage on the farm in New Rochelle granted him by
the New York legislature.*

and have ultimately contributed to the freedom, sovereignty and independence of the United States."

The words pleased him but the gift itself did not. He was never meant to be a farmer. Isolate himself in this rural nowhere? What he really needed was assurance of a steady supply of money. To sell the farm would satisfy that need but make the public think him an ungrateful and greedy wretch. So he rented the property to a tenant farmer, an arrangement that lasted until Paine's death, and kept appealing to the states for cash in the form of a grant or pension.

Again Washington stepped in to help, enlisting Jefferson and Madison to get Virginia to act. "Can nothing be done in our Assembly for poor Paine?" he wrote Madison. "Must the merits and services of *Common Sense* continue to glide down the stream of time unrewarded by this country?"

Madison tried, but the legislature voted against the bill. Washington then appealed to Pennsylvania, and this time it agreed to grant Paine five hundred pounds. Still not satisfied, Washington put pressure on congress. And finally, in October 1785, the federal legislature voted to give Paine $3,000.

It was an extremely generous gift, setting a precedent for the government to honor a writer. Taken together with the income generated by the New Rochelle farm and the money granted by Pennsylvania, it meant Paine could pay his debts. He thought he could live comfortably from now on.

He had long been interested in science and technology from the time he had soaked up lectures by Newtonians in England. Now he was free to develop his own ideas for inventions. Toward the end of 1785 he began to work on a design for a single-span wooden bridge, three hundred feet long, to go across the Harlem River in New York. He took on as his assistant a young artisan, John Hall, newly arrived from England with years of experience on engineering projects. The two men made several bridge models, of wood or of cast iron. Paine wanted a single-span design because bridges standing on piers were often damaged by ice crushes in severe winters.

When the Harlem River project failed to win financial backing, Paine shifted to the design of a wrought-iron single-span bridge to cross the Schuylkill River in Philadelphia. No bridge covered it at that time. Much of 1786 went into these efforts. Just before Christmas, Paine packed his thirteen-foot model on a sled and drew it by horse to the home of Benjamin Franklin, who had come back from France, for a private viewing. Franklin arranged for the model to be displayed in the State House, where much of the town came to see it. The response was so enthusiastic Paine thought a public bridge-building company could be formed to raise the capital for construction. But neither the state nor private investors were ready to take a chance on Paine's invention.

Why not try your innovation abroad, suggested Franklin. Maybe the French would build it across the Seine? Or the English across the Thames?

Meanwhile, Paine became entangled in a fierce controversy over a major economic and political issue. The Bank of North America—the nation's first bank, founded by Robert Morris—was in great trouble. Both the state of Pennsylvania and the congress had granted it a charter. But a bill to repeal its charter had been passed in September 1786 by the Radical majority in the state legislature. The Radicals charged that the bank's directors would acquire such great economic power that they would come to control the state and the government. The bill crippled the bank as European investors complained of bad faith and American depositors withdrew large sums.

Why did the bank concern Paine? Because he believed in both a strong central government and a national bank, even though many of his Radical friends strongly disapproved of both. But Paine said a powerful central government could play a dynamic and creative role in establishing a solid national economy. Through commerce, the various regions of the United States would be linked together. And the benefits of that commerce would cement relations among Americans of different classes, religions, languages, and customs. These views led Paine to support the bank.

In a pamphlet and a series of letters to the press Paine tried to rally pro–bank forces to restore the charter. "The whole community," he wrote, "derives benefit from the operation of the bank."

Many disagreed. The bank's enemies were a mixed lot: some opposed all banks on principle, some feared banks were easily corrupted, some wanted to establish their own bank, some believed the bank favored its friends and denied credit to others.

These were hard times, because the end of the war had brought on a major economic crisis. Farmers, artisans, and merchants had run up debts and wanted easier credit to carry them. They were divided among themselves, however, on whether the bank helped or hindered them by its policies. Many needing credit wanted paper money issued while others feared a flood of paper would launch another round of inflation.

To Paine, paper money was not real money. It was

nothing in itself, only a sign of real wealth that had not yet been produced. It fooled people into thinking they were better off than they actually were. His views were denounced by the Radical majority in the Pennsylvania Assembly who had repealed the bank's charter. It upset him badly to hear himself called traitor and turncoat and a hireling of the rich. Yet he stuck to his convictions, writing that "nothing is more certain than if the bank was destroyed, the market for country produce would be monopolized by a few monied men, who would command the price as they pleased."

For much of 1786 the controversy raged. An editor who had always welcomed Paine's articles refused to publish what he had to say about the bank. Paine replied that "if the freedom of the press is to be determined by the judgement of the editor of a newspaper in preference to that of the people, who when they read will judge for themselves, then freedom is on a very sandy foundation."

Old friends quarreled with him over the issue. Wherever he went, bitter arguments broke out. Although he loved to conduct political debate in print, he hated face-to-face quarrels. In March 1787, a victorious Conservative majority in the state assembly granted a new charter to the Bank of North America. It was cold comfort. Paine felt so abused, so misunderstood, so unappreciated, with no end to it in sight.

The debate over the bank charter revealed how politics was changing. There were as yet no fully formed party system, no political committees or platforms, and only small-scale campaigns for office. Few even thought of politics as a way to get what they wanted. Parties were feared as an instrument to split people into factions. As one hopeful said, let this be a time "when all party and animosity will be absorbed in the general and generous sentiment of promoting the common good."

But by now, in the mid-1780s, that was only talk; political reality was something else. In at least a few states, Pennsylvania among them, people with shared interests were finding out that they would help themselves by acting together. And, they knew, so would others who had different interests.

It was two such groups that clashed over the bank issue, one openly acting like a political party, the other pretending it was not. Robert Morris, the spokesman for rechartering the bank, tried to pose as a gentleman above any crass profit motive, a man concerned only with the public good. But his chief opponent in the legislative debate, William Findley, a weaver from western Pennsylvania, refused to let him get away with that pose. Yes, he said, Morris and his wealthy friends certainly had much at stake in the charter. They had no right to claim they were neutral, acting like umpires deciding what was good for everyone.   The fact that Morris had a personal stake in the outcome was not wrong in itself. Of course Morris wanted to have the issue decided in his favor. But, Findley asserted, Morris had no right to pretend that support of his personal cause was an act of disinterested virtue, while those who opposed him were guided only by selfishness. That's what politics is about, as Findley saw it: the promotion of the interests of this group or that group. Representatives are elected to promote the particular interests and private causes of their constituents. Let's not be hypocritical about it, Findley was saying.

That truth became more and more visible with every succeeding election contest, local, state, or national. What voters must be wary of is politicians who pretend they are only and always concerned with the good of all.

Tom Paine, however, felt he wanted no more of that. He believed his political career was over. From now on he would give all his energy to "the quiet field of science." He made plans to take his bridge design to Europe and, while abroad, visit his parents in Thetford. He asked Franklin for letters introducing him to important French scientists and politicians. For the second time, Franklin was glad to help. He wrote several letters for Paine, indicating, as this passage shows, his high regard:

The bearer of this letter is Mr. Paine, the author of a famous piece entitled "Common Sense," published here with great effect on the minds of the people at the beginning of the revolution. He is an ingenious, honest man; and as such I beg leave to recommend him to your civilities. He carries with him the model of a bridge of a new construction, his own invention.

On April 26, 1787, Paine's ship sailed from New York. One month later, he landed in France.

❖ 14 ❖

REVOLUTION
IN FRANCE

When Paine arrived in Paris he found his reputation had preceded him. People with prestige and power—scientists, reformers, government officials—knew who he was and what he had done. He was welcomed warmly by Lafayette, the war hero, and by Jefferson, America's minister to France. Upon Franklin's recommendation, the French Academy of Sciences asked a committee to study Paine's plan for a bridge.

Paine had high hopes. But engineering in France was more advanced than in America and many other plans for new types of bridges were being examined. Still, it seemed almost a sure thing when the committee concluded that "Mr. Paine's iron bridge is ingeniously conceived; that its construction is simple, sound, and fit to provide the strength necessary to withstand effects arising from loading; and that it is worthy of a trial."

It never got the trial. As often happens in matters of large investment, politics and patronage may overcome merit. Government backing went instead to a Frenchman's design for a masonry bridge over the Seine.

What about trying his bridge in England? Franklin stood high with its Royal Society. So Paine sent his bridge model to the society's president, and then crossed over from France to visit his mother and old friends in Thetford. He arranged for his mother to receive a regular weekly sum for the rest of her life. (His father had died nearly a year earlier.)

Paine would travel back and forth between France and England for the next several years, splitting his energy between promoting his bridge and politicking. At one point he said he would "rather erect the longest arch in the world than be the greatest emperor in it." He managed to secure patents for his bridge design in England but had great trouble raising the money to construct it. After many false starts, in May 1790, an experimental arch was put up in a London field. A stream of visitors came to view it, but the press ignored it and no investors offered financing. Finally, in October, Paine gave up and had the arch taken down.

Back he went into politics, full-time now.

Of course he could never be indifferent to the great political changes taking place in the world, especially in England and France. He kept an eye on America too. In May 1787, only a few weeks after he had sailed for Europe, the Continental Congress had met in Philadelphia. The delegates threw aside the old Articles of Confederation and wrote a completely new Constitution. Long an advocate of a stronger central government, Paine saw his cause triumph in the new Constitution.

Like Jefferson, he worried over the failure of the convention to include a Bill of Rights. Protecting civil liberties was an ancient English tradition, going back to the Magna Carta of 1215. Americans had often cited English rights when protesting arbitrary acts of the king's officials. When he saw that the draft of the Constitution had no such protection Jefferson said that a Bill of Rights "is what the people are entitled to against every government on earth...and what no just government should refuse."

As the first Congress convened that September, a heated debate took place over constitutional amendments embodying a Bill of Rights, proposed by James Madison. Only the promise of their adoption finally settled the outcome. In June 1788, the states ratified the Constitution and it went into effect. Now every citizen was guaranteed freedoms no government could take away.

As Paine followed the debate over the American

Constitution, he witnessed the beginnings of a great upheaval in France. The nation lived under an absolute monarchy. Its aristocracy was supported by privilege and wealth. Vast tracts of land were controlled by what was still a feudal system. A merchant class had climbed to wealth and felt it ought to share in political power too. The government administration was riddled with corrupt office-holders who made themselves rich. The huge mass of peasants were legally free but still bound by services and obligations to the lords of the land. And in the cities, artisans and workers of all occupations swarmed in the streets and tenements, barely able to survive but for cheap bread.

Everyone below the monarchy and nobility had reason to want social and political change. When a series of economic crises shook France in the 1770s and 1780s, it brought that demand to fever pitch. Under great pressure the government at last permitted freedom of criticism. Political poster blazoned the walls and political caricatures peppered the press. Royal authority cracked under the force of public opinion. Demands for social justice outpaced the government's cautious moves toward mild reforms.

In the summer and fall of 1788, Jefferson saw riots in the streets and the killing of demonstrators by Paris guards. Martial law was imposed by the government. Then the king summoned a National Assembly—for the first time in 175 years—to meet at Versailles in May 1789.

The result was electric. The news roused hope of a national rebirth in the peasants and the people of the towns. A great stream of pamphlets and petitions and news sheets voicing the exciting new ideas and ridiculing the old regime poured from the presses. One of the most important of them was a pamphlet by Abbé Emmanuel-Joseph Sieyes, which for the first time declared that the middle class, acting for the people as a whole, was ready to take over the government, whether the nobility wished to join it or not.

A bitterly cold winter came on, making things even worse. The king, desperately short of money, was unable to supply the starving and freezing poor with bread or fuel.

Masses of the unemployed took to the streets, crying out for work.

Somehow Paine, who was away in England during these violent days, expected more from Louis XVI than he ever had from George III. Hadn't Louis given magnificent support to the American Revolution? Paine didn't think the French monarch a tyrant so hungry for power that he would refuse to share it with others. As Louis made concessions to public opinion, Paine thought he meant gradually to loosen the tight controls of the old regime. He hoped the king would manage to make his way toward a constitutional monarchy—a republic under a king with limited powers. Paine even wrote to Washington that the king "prides himself on being at the head of the revolution."

But on July 14, 1789, the people of Paris stormed the fortress called the Bastille. The violence of revolution had

The storming of the fortress called the Bastille marked the opening of the French Revolution.

begun. The capture of the Bastille marked the real opening of the French Revolution. Princes, aristocrats, and ministers fled the country. That summer, out in the provinces, the peasants revolted, burned the landlords' châteaux, and began to execute officials. The National Assembly—made up of the middle class, the clergy, and liberal aristocrats—responded by taking the first decisive step to dismantle the old feudal system of land tenure. Late in August the assembly adopted a Declaration of Rights. "The death certificate of the old regime," observed Jefferson.

Without ideas, without answer to the questions troubling people, a revolution would hardly be possible. We've seen how Tom Paine's ideas percolated through the American mind and helped bring about decisive change. Where do ideas come from? The French middle class drew mainly from the writings of their eighteenth-century thinkers—chiefly Rousseau and Montesquieu and Voltaire. Through such teaching, they learned to proclaim the principles of the "Rights of Man" and "Popular Sovereignty." The masses of the peasants and the city poor soaked up the same body of ideas. You could see it and hear it in their slogans and actions in the months before the fall of the Bastille. Of course the peasants joined in the Revolution with their traditional demand for land and an end to feudal dues and taxes, and the city people with their demand for a just price for bread. The ideas of the French writers shaped a new consciousness that the old way of life was as unjust in its principles as it was terrible in its effects.

Tom Paine, back in Paris from November 1789 till the following March, spoke up at lively gatherings where revolutionary strategy and tactics were debated. Among the group were French leaders like Lafayette and Condorcet and such foreigners as Jefferson, Franklin, and Scottish economist Adam Smith. The experience of the American Revolution (everyone had read Paine in translation) was discussed to see how it might serve as a useful guide in the French Revolution. Lafayette, turned revolutionary politician, was a powerful influence now. He founded political clubs and, serving in the National Assembly, introduced a number of reforms. Church lands were nationalized, the royal veto suspended, and several feudal laws abolished.

But Paine, close to Lafayette as friend and counselor, felt the marquis was holding back from extending democracy to the fullest. Lafayette's supporters wanted a constitutional monarchy in which the Parliament was dominant over King and Church. But the majority of the population were denied political rights. Only those who could afford to pay a certain amount of taxes could vote or hold office. In effect, these laws split the nation in two. Everyone had full citizenship rights, but money or the lack of it limited political rights for all too many.

Still, for about two years, the Revolution kept moving away from absolutism and toward greater democracy. For a while the new constitutional monarchy seemed fairly stable. The European powers, none of them democratic, watched the Revolution nervously, fearing their own people might draw lessons from France.

England was one of those powers. Though it had a Parliament and a Bill of Rights, it knew its people had many grievances against the government. And as Paine moved back and forth across the English Channel, British spies kept a close eye on this firebrand.

❖ 15 ❖

THE RIGHTS

OF MAN

On his trips back to England in the late 1780s, Paine renewed his friendships with the reformers. They had supported the American struggle for independence and now honored him for his great role in it. Their own efforts at reform, however, had slackened in recent years. But the outbreak of the French Revolution revitalized them and transformed English politics. If the French could create a new progressive order almost overnight, why couldn't the English change their institutions as quickly?

Paine had long wanted to apply the principles of *Common Sense* to English conditions. As early as 1778 he had thought of sneaking secretly into England and spreading propaganda against the British war on America. Only the fear of being caught and executed as a spy caused him to drop the plan. Nevertheless, he clung to the idea of writing a plea for democracy in England. As his book got under way, he heard that his friend, the reformer Edmund Burke, had been so shocked by the events in France that he had begun writing a book to denounce it as a terrible catastrophe. It was hard to believe, for Burke had boldly backed the American cause in its early years and only yesterday was trying to help Paine secure support for his bridge.

When Burke's book, *Reflections on the Revolution in France*, appeared in November 1790, Paine reshaped his own work The *Rights of Man*, into an attack on Burke.

Burke's book was hugely successful in Tory circles, for it voiced the fears and suspicions of radicalism the upper class had long felt and provided a rationale for opposing political change.

The *Rights of Man* appeared in March 1791, a few months after the publication of Burke's book. It was dedicated to George Washington, now in his first term as president. While Burke spoke in pompous tones to the narrow audience of the upper class, Paine embraced the entire nation as his readers. And again, as in his American writings, he used a forceful, vivid, common language that captivated his public.

In *Rights* Paine explained the events of the French Revolution, showing how progressive these were as against Burke's depiction of them as unspeakably evil. Angered by Burke's sympathy for the French ruling class and his indifference to its victims, Paine wrote:

> *Not one glance of compassion, not one commiserating reflection, that I can find throughout his book, has he bestowed on those who lingered out the most wretched of lives, a life without hope, in the most miserable of prisons.... He is not affected by the reality of distress touching the heart, but by the showy resemblage of it striking his imagination. He pities the plumage, but forgets the dying bird.*

To Burke, the French people making a revolution were the "swinish multitude." He was just as nasty about the English artisan class Paine represented. Hairdressers and candlemakers, he conceded, ought not to suffer oppression from the state, but if such people are permitted to rule, "the state suffers oppression."

Comparing the new French system of government with the present English one, Paine showed how bad the English system was. Hard facts: In 1790, only five percent of the total English population of eight million could vote. With that tiny an electorate, just six thousand voters—a majority of the voters in 129 districts—put 257 men into Parliament. And these made up the majority of the House of Commons! Fifty of these same Members of Parliament were elected by a mere 340 voters.

Though it still had some limitations, the French suffrage was much broader. The National Assembly met often, not once in seven years like the British Parliament. And it was based on equal electoral districts, not "rotten boroughs." The French guaranteed freedom of conscience; in England, religious dissenters faced all kinds of barriers.

The English movement for Parliamentary reform had begun while Paine was still a young corset maker in Thetford. But it became widely popular only now, under the example of the French revolutionaries. And *Rights* powerfully propelled the movement forward.

Paine's political ideas, expressed simple and clearly, made their appeal widely effective. He took up two basic questions: what is the source of government, and for what purpose is it created? He reaffirmed the principle that a constitution must be made by the people. It is not created by the act of government; the people create the government.

Burke, on the other hand, held that the sovereign state of England and its Constitution came out of the remote past and that custom and precedent, piled up over the long centuries, should never be tampered with. Englishmen knew their place, he said, and by nature favored the past. What was this "swinish" business about the "rights of man" and "democracy?" "We fear God," he went on, "we look up with awe to kings; with affection to parliaments; with duty to magistrates; with reverence to priests; and with respect to nobility."

Burke's view was that government is "a partnership not only between those who are living, but between those who are living, those who are dead, and those who are to be born."

Edmund Burke, British statesman and orator, whose book attacking the French Revolution was countered by Paine's work The Rights of Man.

No, said Paine:

> *Every age and generation must be free to act for itself in all cases as the ages and generations which preceded it. The vanity and presumption of governing beyond the grave is the most ridiculous and insolent of all tyrannies.... Every generation is, and must be, competent to all the purposes which its occasions require. It is the living, and not the dead, that are to be accommodated.*

This was the central argument in *Rights*. Paine had touched on it in *Common Sense* and later, in 1786, had said:

*As we are not to live forever ourselves,
and other generations are to follow us, we
have neither the power not the right to
govern them, or to say how they shall govern themselves. It is the summit of human
vanity, and shows a covetousness of power
beyond the grave, to be dictating to the
world to come.*

Paine's view of the world was vastly different from Burke's. Except for America, Paine wrote, all other nations live under the rule of despotism. Monarchs like George III make people fear to think for themselves. To criticize the government publicly is to invite the charge of treason. To exercise your natural rights—your God-given rights to freedom of speech, of assembly, of religion—is to invite persecution and imprisonment.

Living under despotism makes you dependent on the whims and wishes of others—of the rulers and their officials, their toadies, their favorites. They treat you like dumb animals to be herded wherever they choose. When you are always told what to do, how to do it, and when to do it, you forget who you really are. You no longer are your own true self. Nature has fitted you to be a citizen, but despots have made you into a subject. All power, all property, all prestige is theirs. You, in their eyes, are a nothing.

Paine thought that despotism not only crippled personality and poisoned human relations but was the cause of bloody conflicts between states. Until the eighteenth century many had believed war was inevitable, part of human fate, as natural as earthquakes or floods. But Paine, like other thinkers of his time, had begun to see war not as a necessity but as an event that could be avoided. In *Rights* he portrayed despotism as a system that bred plots and quarrels, rivalries and enmities, greed and violence. Rulers taxed their subjects heavily to pay for war with their neighbors. War was a despot's way to extend his power over others, as well as over his own people.

Then how to stop war? How to end despotism? How

to create a society of peace and plenty? Could it be done through "reason and accommodation" or were bloody convulsions bound to happen? Paine had confidence in the ability of people to bring about change. "What is there in the world but man?" he asked. Man, he said, needs "at all times to watch against the attempted encroachment of power, and to prevent its running to excess."

Burke's preaching of obedience to power was not for him. The power of government should be in the hands of the people, who entrust power to elected officials and who can take back that power at any time by withdrawing their consent.

Paine gave the manuscript of Part I of *Rights* to a London printer. As the pages came off the press, government agents dropped into the print shop, on the watch for what that seditious Paine was doing. Frightened by their queries, the printer stopped the job dead. He was not ready to risk jail. Paine packed the unbound sheets into a cart and hauled them to another printer, borrowing money from a friend to pay for the work. He left completion of the publication process to other friends and then hurried off to Paris to arrange for French translation and publication.

Once off press in England, and then in translation in France and other parts of Europe, *The Rights of Man* became an overnight best-seller. Critics hailed it as a "wonderful work." Nowhere was the response greater than in England, Paine's prime target. His defense of the French Revolution, his exposure of Burke's reactionary beliefs, and his attack upon the British system of government, created a fierce public debate over fundamental political principles.

In America, sections of *Rights* quickly appeared in several newspapers, and the book itself, with an unauthorized preface by Jefferson, then Washington's secretary of state, came out in May 1971. Paine sent fifty copies to Washington, to whom the book was dedicated. But the president, beset by a struggle between left and right in his administration, was embarrassed by the gift and delayed ten months in thanking Paine.

Now, two hundred years later, Professor John Keane

MAD TOM.
or the MAN *of* RIGHTS.

British cartoon ridiculing Paine for his book, The Rights of Man.

holds that *The Rights of Man* has "proved to be one of those rare books of great political insight that outlive their time and place of birth."

Naturally, Paine rejoiced to find himself in the limelight. But the book would cause him great suffering. The intimidation of his printer was a sign of what was to come. He would be tailed by secret agents, vilified by government propaganda, smeared by malicious gossips. He once wrote that "truth is always ultimately victorious." That did not mean the teller of truth would always be blessed with happiness.

Of course *Rights* provoked loud protest too. It was called "vulgar," "coarse," "uncouth," "wild." Still, it sold and sold and sold, even at the high price of three shillings. In two months fifty thousand copies were sold in England alone. This when the average sale of a novel was 1250 copies, and about half that for a work of nonfiction. By the end of ten years, some half million copies of Rights had been sold in England, whose literate population was only four million. Like *Common Sense* fifteen years earlier, *Rights* was read aloud to people unable to read and talked about everywhere. Discussions of the book at meetings of reform or radical groups brought loud cheers for Paine and tributes to him for this "most masterly book." "It seemed to electrify the nation," one radical recalled. A London tailor announced in a pub that "Tom Paine was the only one to save this country and the whole world," while a pamphlet termed him "a God: compared to princes, lords, bishops, and judges." Spies prowling the taverns to gather intelligence reported toasts like "Death to the King and Parliament and Success to Tom Paine!" When requests for cheaper editions came in, Paine happily consented, and as usual, gave up all royalties.

Meanwhile, in Paris arranging for a French edition, Paine drew up plans for a sequel to *Rights*.

It would be Paine's boldest and greatest work.

❖ 16 ❖

TO DO AWAY WITH POVERTY

As Paine observed the world around him, everywhere he saw people discontented, most of them living in misery. "When in countries that we call civilized," he wrote, "we see age going to the workhouse and youth to the gallows, something must be wrong in the system of government."

In writing Part II of *The Rights of Man*, he wanted to lay out the general principles of government and society. By examining them afresh, he hoped to get at the causes of human unhappiness and to find ways to remedy them.

Looking at criminal justice, he asked, "Why is it that scarcely any are executed but the poor?" He answered, "Lack of education for the young and a decent livelihood for the old." In other words, the government did nothing to provide the conditions that can make people happy. Could you expect anything different in England? No, for its government was run by the representatives of special privilege and special interests. But why should a legislature be composed entirely of the rich, rather than of those who bake the bread, brew the beer, and hire out their labor power?

Again, as in *Common Sense*, he ridiculed King George and the system of hereditary monarchy. Take England's monarchy, he said. It began when "a band of ruffians" overran the land (in the Norman invasion of 1066) and then allowed the chief ruffian to change the name of ruffian to king.

Instead of a monarchy, people needed a "republican

government." By that he meant simply "government established and constituted for the interest of the public." All the citizens cannot sit in legislatures and make the laws. That would hardly be practical. It is more convenient for the voters to choose their own legislators to represent them in government.

This is how the republican government of the United States of America is constituted, he went on. And then, idealizing the results of the young democracy, he asserted:

> *There the poor are not oppressed, the rich are not privileged, industry is not mortified by the splendid extravagance of a court rioting at its expense. Their taxes are few, because their government is just; and as there is nothing to render them wretched, there is nothing to engender riots and tumults.*

Praising the French Revolution, Paine compared it favorably with the evils of the British system, where progressive change was all but impossible. He wrote:

> *Government ought to be as much open to improvement as anything which pertains to man, instead of which it has been monopolized from age to age by the most ignorant and vicious of the human race. Need we any other proof of their wretched management than the excess of debts and taxes with which every nation groans, and the quarrels into which they have precipitated the world?*

But Paine was not content with advocating reform of government. He went much further. Once a truly democratic government is established by the people what should its goal be? "It ought to have no other object than the general happiness," he wrote. "When instead of this, it operates to create and increase wretchedness in any of the parts of society, it is on a wrong system and reformation is necessary."

It is time to do away with poverty, he wrote. Any republican government should adopt an economic program that would serve the needs of the mass of its people. Paine then outlined a policy of social welfare that went far beyond what was known in his day. He set a course for the social legislation of the twentieth century.

Paine's plan called for free public education, for the relief of the poor, for old-age pensions, for cash benefits to be given at birth and at marriage, and for government-provided jobs and housing to assist the unemployed and immigrants. He urged increases in salaries for excise officers, the lower clergy, and soldiers and sailors.

To pay for the operation of his social welfare plan, Paine proposed a graduated income tax. That is, the greater one's income, the larger the percentage of it to be taxed.

And why not? The taxes of most Englishmen, he said, could be reduced if the government stopped making war and stopped paying huge pensions to members of the aristocracy. Recalling the pension paid to just one aristocrat, he wrote:

> *It is inhuman to talk of a million sterling a year, paid out of the public taxes of any country, for the support of any individual, while thousands, who are forced to contribute thereto, are pinned from want, and struggling with misery. Government does not consist in contrast between prisons and palace, between poverty and pomp, it is not instituted to rob the needy of his mite, and increase the wretchedness of the wretched.*

Paine also had ideas for bringing about peaceful relations among the nations. He advocated treaties between England, France, the United States, and Holland to reduce by half the size of their war fleets. Differences and conflicts could be settled by international arbitration. It was one of the early proposals heading in the direction of creating the United Nations.

Part II of *The Rights of Man*, dedicated to Paine's friend Lafayette, was published in February 1792. That book, said historian Eric Foner, "marked a turning point in the history

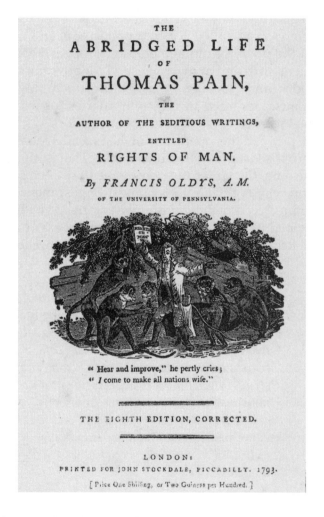

Title page of the first—and most hostile—biography of Paine, written under the pseudonym Francis Oldys by George Chalmers, a lawyer loyal to the Crown, which commissioned the book.

of English radicalism. Paine was the first to provide a social program for the English reform movement, to make the traditional demands for Parliamentary reform meaningful to the daily lives of the middle class and workingmen."

The English government, already worried by the rapid growth of lower-class radicalism, was shaken by the impact of this new volume. Tories panicked at Paine's proposal for progressive taxation on inheritances to distribute the wealth and to pay for a broad program of social welfare.

The British ruling class was convinced, writes Oxford University professor Isaiah Berlin, "that the working man was a savage unprincipled brute who naturally thirsted to overturn a society so obviously not to his advantage."

The government wanted to take no chances with what Paine might do with those "brutes." It did everything it could to suppress a budding revolutionary movement. It censored the press. It suspended the Habeas Corpus Act. It arrested radical leaders, charged them with high treason or sedition, and gave them savage sentences of deportation to the penal colonies. Any attempt to organize workers into clubs or societies or unions was labeled "conspiracy" and banned.

Mobs were organized by the king's friends to take to the streets and break up rallies. They attacked the homes of prominent democrats. The scientist Joseph Priestley saw his house sacked and his scientific equipment, books, and papers destroyed.

To ruin Paine's reputation the king's men hired a London lawyer, George Chalmers, to write a hostile biography under the pen name of Francis Oldys. It smeared Paine as a bad husband, a failed shopkeeper, a dishonest exciseman, and an atheist. The book sold well, as that kind of scandalous biography usually does. The layer of muck would cling to Paine long after he died.

Paine chose not to answer the lies but pursued a quiet life—writing, meeting with friends, playing dominoes or chess in the evenings, or passing the time in conversation, which, a friend said, "was always enlightened, full of information, entertainment and anecdote."

Paine's optimism, his unbounded faith in what people could do when they were awakened, he clung to tenaciously. Look across the sea, he would cry. The American democracy exists, and it is flourishing! See what the people of France are doing! Yes, there are other ways to live and govern! His pen ignited long-dormant discontent and made his readers believe that something better could be won.

He gave to the English people a new language of radical egalitarianism. His influence was felt immediately by the young English poets. William Wordsworth, in July 1790, set off with a companion to walk through France on the first anniversary of the fall of the Bastille. Remembering, a few years later, a "hunger-bitten" peasant girl they had encountered, he wrote these lines:

> *...and at the sight my friend*
> *In agitation said, "'Tis against that*
> *That we are fighting," I with him believed*
> *That a benignant spirit was abroad*
> *Which might not be withstood, that poverty*
> *Abject as this would in a little time*
> *Be found no more, that we should see the earth*
> *Unthwarted in her wish to recompense*
> *The meek, the lowly, patient child of toil,*
> *All institutes for ever blotted out*
> *That legalised exclusion, empty pomp*
> *Abolished, sensual state and cruel power,*
> *Whether by edict of the one or few;*
> *And finally, as sum and crown of all,*
> *Should see the people having a strong hand*
> *In framing their own laws; whence better days*
> *To all mankind.*

There were English radicals who went far beyond Paine in promoting the wholesale revolutionary overthrow of institutions. But, as English historian E. P. Thompson points out, Paine's writing

> *did not challenge the property rights of the*

*rich.... In terms of political democracy he
wished to level all inherited distinctions
and privileges; but he gave no counte-
nance to economic levelling. In political
rights every man must have equal rights
as a citizen: in economic society he must
naturally remain employer or employed,
and the State should not interfere with the
capital of the one or the wages of the
other.... The aristocracy were the main target; their property might be threatened...
and their rents regarded as a feudal exact-
ing...but—however hard trade unionists
might fight under their employers—
industrial capital was assumed to be the
fruit of enterprise and beyond reach of
political intrusion.*

It is easy now, two hundred years later, to see that
Paine had a romantic view of human nature and could not
foresee the future. He could even write that "I do not
believe that Monarchy and Aristocracy will continue seven
years longer in any of the enlightened countries in
Europe." How could he know that a Napoleon, a
Mussolini, a Stalin, a Hitler, and all too many other dictators were down the road?

Nor did Paine understand the nature of the system of
private enterprise. He wrote at a time when the Industrial
Revolution had already begun. But he did not grasp how
competitive it was. That the need to capture greater shares
of the market and to accumulate more profits would
become pressure for paying as little as possible to those
whom one employed. Even if he sensed the danger, he
overrated the power and the willingness of the exploited to
defend themselves. And he did not allow for the possibili-
ty that even a government democratically elected, which
was supposed to protect the people's rights and serve their
needs, would be more strongly influenced by the rich and
powerful than by the common voter.

William Blake, the English artist, poet, was a friend of Paine.
He warned Paine that the British were going to arrest him.

The degree of Paine's radicalism did not matter to the British government. It was unrelenting in its attacks. In 1792 it announced it would try him for seditious libel. Warned by the poet William Blake to flee at once, Paine went to the port of Dover. Somehow he got by the customs officials and boarded a ship for France. A few minutes later government agents arrived to arrest him. Although Paine had escaped, the government went ahead and, without Paine present, tried him for writing *The Rights of Man*. He was convicted and declared an outlaw. If he should ever return, he could be sentenced to life imprisonment or even executed.

On September 13, 1792, he was once again in France. He never returned to England.

❖ 17 ❖

REIGN OF TERROR

W hile Paine was in England, hounded by the government, the French people claimed him as their champion. In August 1792 the National Assembly declared Paine a full citizen of France. It honored him and fifteen other foreigners "for their writings and their courage in the cause of liberty."

Soon, even before he arrived in France, he was one of two foreigners elected to the National Convention. "Come, friend of the people," the Convention wrote him, "to swell the number of patriots in an assembly which will decide the destiny of the human race. The happy period you have predicted for the nation has arrived. Come!"

When he reached Paris, he checked in at White's Hotel, on a tiny side street. It was the nesting place of a group of ardent English, Irish, and American francophiles. (Within three months, caught between the two fires of revolution and reaction, the group would be scattered, some arrested, imprisoned, executed.) Paine was welcomed by the group of émigrés and by the circle of English-speaking French friends he had met on earlier visits. They were moderate republicans, their thinking close to his own. Supporters of the Revolution had already begun to divide into groups, not quite yet political parties, but with different ideas about where the Revolution should go. Paine's friends were leaders of the group known as the Girondins, because some of them came from the Gironde region in southwestern France. They were men of property, lawyers, merchants, former aristocrats, remote from the raw democracy of the Paris streets.

To the left of the Girondins were the Jacobins, whose name derived from an order of Jacobin monks in whose abandoned library they used to meet. The Jacobins grew rapidly, establishing branches in the provinces, recruiting half a million members and perhaps as many sympathizers. Maximilien Robespierre, a young provincial lawyer, became their leader. The Jacobins were willing to use ruthless force to secure ends that they believed good. They were an early example of how an organized and indoctrinated minority can impose itself upon a country in a time of crisis.

When Paine took his seat in the National Convention, he was placed on a committee to create a constitution for the new republic. Paine helped prepare the initial draft, modeling it on the Pennsylvania Constitution of 1776. It was prefaced by a Declaration of the Rights of Man. The idea for it was first proposed by Lafayette and drafted by him with the help of both Jefferson and Paine. It is a manifesto comparable in importance to Jefferson's Declaration of Independence. It begins with the statement that "the natural rights of man, civil and political, are liberty, equality, security, property, social protection and resistance to oppression." Freedom of thought, speech, the press, religion are all guaranteed. Every citizen is held to be equally in need of education, and the society owes it to them to provide it. There must be taxes, but only for "the general welfare and to meet public needs." Finally, the people always have the right to reform and alter the constitution.

When the committee Paine served on completed its work in early 1793, the draft constitution was presented to the convention. But discussion of it never took place. The reason? France had been thrown into a state of chaos. The country was now at war with England, Holland, Spain, Austria, and Prussia. The rulers of those states, monarchs all, feared for their own fate if their people were inspired to follow the example of France in getting rid of its monarchy.

Step by step, beginning with the fall of the Bastille, Louis XVI had been forced to give up power. He had accepted the first constitution in the fall of 1791. But secretly he had sent messages to monarchs abroad asking for military help to restore him to power. Then, trying to flee the country, he had been captured and forced to return. In September 1792 the monarchy was abolished and the republic proclaimed.

Finally, a few weeks later, the king was indicted for treason before the full convention in which Paine sat. All the delegates, including Paine, voted him guilty. Paine, who had always opposed capital punishment, pleaded that the king's life be spared. No one was criminal enough, he argued, for the barbarity of the death penalty. Besides, he urged, although they all knew the king's grave faults, he had, after all, "aided my much beloved America to break its chains." Don't act in the spirit of revenge but in the spirit of justice, Paine pleaded. Don't send him to the guillotine. Imprison him instead, until the war ends, and then exile him to America.

To show mercy would win favor abroad, he argued. Although the Girondins supported Paine, the king, by a slim majority, was sentenced to death. He was beheaded before a crowd of twenty thousand people on the public square known today as the Place de la Concorde.

Paine saw the execution as a turning point. He predicted that the violence turned upon the king would be turned on those who had opposed his execution. He told a friend that the king's death was "a signal for my departure, for I will not abide such sanguinary men."

At last he had opened his eyes to the dark side of revolution, the side Edmund Burke had written about. When Paine had come to live in France a year earlier, he had still held the utopian belief that revolutions transformed human beings, that in remaking their society and its institutions they remade themselves. What he did not foresee was that under the intense pressure of changing their world, people come to differ passionately about how to do it. They split into factions, quarreling viciously over methods and meanings. They call one another nasty names—cowards, turncoats, traitors, betrayers. Decency in human relationships disappears as the struggle for power accelerates. In the end, with confusion and demoralization threatening to restore the old regime, a minority can take over, using ruthless violence to consolidate control.

That was happening in France. A struggle for power among the various groups within the revolutionary movement had culminated in the dominance of the Jacobins, especially in two committees they controlled. The committees set up to combat counterrevolutionary threats to the regime, to raise new armies to fight the enemies of France, and to regulate the economy. There had been uprisings in the provinces by peasants still discontent with what the new government had done for them. In Paris, mobs incited by Jacobin newspapers had broken into the prisons and murdered hundreds of inmates accused of being royalists. The massacres horrified the Girondins, who pleaded for the restoration of law and order.

Some of the mob action was spontaneous violence. But organized terror came into use as the struggle for power intensified among the various factions. The Jacobin party introduced the idea of planned violence to smash any opposition to their policy. In what came to be known as the Reign of Terror (1793–94) an army of informers was recruited to round up anyone under the faintest suspicion of anti-Jacobin sentiments. The Terror was carried from Paris into the provinces, and great numbers of suspects were butchered without trial. In one district, victims were chained together and shot at with cannon. The wounded were finished off with bullets; the dead buried in mass graves of quicklime. At Nantes, five thousand were put to death by mass drownings in the river Loire. Women, children, old people were raped, mutilated, killed without mercy. Some were buried alive. The French scholar Jean-Clement Martin holds that the total loss in one region was a quarter of a million—one third its entire population. He describes it as "a human catastrophe of colossal proportions."

Twenty-one of the leading Girondins, men Paine had known well, were among those executed. Historians estimate that in addition to the mass slaughters, another 400,000 men, women, and children were imprisoned in dungeons. (Large as these numbers were, they pale in comparison with the huge loss of lives caused by the policies of Stalin, Hitler, Mao, Pol Pot, and other dictators of the twentieth century.)

France was the first country in which terrorism was used as a method of preventive repression. Not only did individuals come under suspicion, but whole classes, groups, and parties were labeled potential enemies of the Revolution. Another innovation was terrorization of thought. The people in power tried to control ideas, art, literature, and the press by censorship, by intimidation, by terror.

They called it "revolutionary justice." But it was exercised not by courts, not by jury trial, but upon the mere whim or will of the people in power. They murdered anyone they chose in the name of the collective good of the people. The politics of the revolutionaries in power decided who would live and who would die. The revolutionary leaders took unto themselves the right to determine what the people wanted and to carry that out.

In the name of a "sacred mission" thousands were ruined, tortured, murdered. When the White Terror (meaning from the political right wing) took over, it continued the killing, only this time of the Red (left-wing) terrorists. In the end, the original revolutionary leaders themselves fell one after another at the guillotine. What had begun as a movement of liberation turned into butchery by rival terrorists. The final outcome was a coup that made Napoléon military dictator of France and turned the Republic into the empire.

In April 1793, Paine wrote to Thomas Jefferson, who was back home serving as Washington's secretary of state. Admitting his disappointment in the course the Revolution was taking, Paine said, "Had this revolution been conducted consistently with its principles, there was once a good prospect of extending liberty through the greatest part of Europe; but I now relinquish that hope."

Seeking a refuge from the turmoil of Paris, Paine moved to Saint-Denis, a village just north of the city. There he took three rooms in a quiet hotel, with spacious gardens he could walk in. We catch a glimpse of his everyday life from an old friend, Clio Rickman, a poet and painter Paine had known in Lewes, who came over to stay with him in the summer of 1793:

> *He usually rose about seven. After break-fast he usually stayed an hour or two in the garden, where he one morning pointed out the kind of spider whose web fur-nished him with the first idea of con-structing his iron bridge (a final model of which, in mahogany, is preserved in Paris). The little happy circle who lived with him will ever remember those days with delight: with these select friends he would talk of his boyish days, play at chess, whist, piquet, or cribbage, and enliven the moments by many interesting anecdotes; with these he would play at marbles, scotch hops, battledores, etc, on the broad and fine gravel walk at the upper end of his garden, and then retire to his boudoir, where he was up to his knees in letters and papers of various descrip-tions. Here he remained till dinner time; and unless he visited Brissot's family, or some particular friend, in the evening, which was his frequent custom, he joined again the society of his favourites and fel-low-boarders, with whom his conversation was often witty and cheerful, always acute and improving, but never frivolous. Incorrupt, straightforward and sincere, he pursued his political course in France, as everywhere else, let the government or clamour or faction of the day be what it might, with firmness, with clearness, and without a shadow of turning.*

Georg Forster, a German scientist visiting Paine, reported, "He is better in print than in the flesh. He has all the wit and egotism of the model Englishman. His blazing-red face dotted with purple blotches make him ugly, although he appears inspired and his eyes are full of fire."

Writing again to Jefferson, after the guillotining of Girondins, Paine still did not denounce the Revolution. He told Jefferson that France could not carry the Revolution into Europe, nor could the combined powers conquer France. He believed each side wanted peace, but neither, out of pride, would ask for it. So he hoped Jefferson could persuade Congress to send a mission to negotiate a truce. Nothing came of that.

In another letter, this time to Danton, a Jacobin leader, Paine warned of the dangers of the centralization of power

Georges-Jacques Danton, called the "Giant" of the French Revolution, was himself declared guilty of treason and executed. "Where will it all end?" he asked.

and the ruthless forcing of rapid change upon the nation:

> *I am exceedingly disturbed at the distrac-*
> *tions, jealousies, discontents and uneasi-*
> *ness that reign among us, and which, if*
> *they continue, will bring ruin and dis-*
> *grace upon the Republic.... I am distressed*
> *to see matters so badly conducted, and so*
> *little attention paid to moral principles. It*
> *is these things that injure the character of*
> *the Revolution and discourage the*
> *progress of liberty all over the world.*

Then, taking account of the deliberate campaigns of rumors, false charges, denunciations, and vilification launched by radical factions against one another, he said: "If every individual is to indulge his private malignancy or his private ambition, to denounce at random and without any kind of proof, all confidence will be undermined and all authority destroyed."

On June 2, 1793, the Jacobins seized power at gunpoint in the convention. The Republic was dead. France was now in the hands of a dictatorship. Girondins, all moderates, were denounced as "enemies of the Revolution." The district that had elected Paine to the convention (he had by now stopped attending it) declared that he had "lost their confidence."

He kept out of sight, sticking to his hotel in Saint-Denis. He felt himself choked by an ever-tightening noose of suspicion. Unable to block out his fears, he couldn't eat or sleep. He struggled with a terrible choice: If he worked with the Jacobin regime, he would be sacrificing his principles and would sooner or later find himself attacked as a "traitor to the Revolution." Yet if he refused to collaborate, he would be suspected of being an enemy.

The Jacobins surprised him by asking his advice on how to get America to send large shipments of badly needed food to France. He agreed to help and for several weeks tried to make arrangements. At the same time, he made secret plans to leave France, to escape the threat to his personal safety. Cautious as he was, rumors about his disloyalty circulated, and on the floor of the convention a Jacobin deputy read out his name on an official list of "traitors to the Revolution." He was described as one of the strongest supporters of Louis XVI and as a native of France's leading enemy, England.

As the Terror spread and his own fate hung on a thread, Paine tried to divert himself by tackling a new project. He had already made some notes for a pamphlet meant to be a vindication of pure religion. (We will discuss it later.) Meanwhile, the Jacobins were working the public up to a hatred for all foreigners, especially the English. Late one night, two of Paine's English friends, staying in his hotel, were arrested by armed agents and taken off to prison.

On Christmas Eve, 1793, Paine went into Paris for dinner with American friends at White's Hotel. Too tired to go home, he stayed in the hotel overnight. In the morning, he was awakened by banging on his door. The police rushed in to search his room for suspicious papers. Finding nothing, they took Paine to his Saint-Denis apartment where they ransacked his rooms, gathered up all his books and papers, including the manuscript pages of *The Age of Reason*, and then carried him off to prison.

❖ 18 ❖

A PRISON CELL

"I know nothing so cruel as to wake up in a prison cell, in a place where the most horrible dream is less horrible than reality."

That was how one Frenchman recalled the months he spent in a Paris prison at the end of 1793. Paine, too, was locked in a cell in one of the fifty buildings converted hastily into prisons to house seven thousand people arrested on the flimsiest pretexts that December.

His prison was the Palais de Luxembourg. Once the splendid home of nobility, it was now the decrepit "antechamber of death," for the great majority of political suspects would go quickly to the guillotine.

Paine was thrust into a small ground-floor cell, eight by ten feet, with one boarded-up window. It had a straw mattress and one chair. Through the brick floor, level with the earth outside, water oozed up after every rainfall. The vermin-infested cells stank of filth, excrement, and sickness.

He often lay awake nights, unable to sleep for the crying and moaning coming from neighboring cells or the shrieking of the condemned as they were herded down the corridors toward death. With a candle to light the dark, he would read in his cell. Sometimes, blocking fear of what might happen to him, he would take up his quill and write.

He managed to produce a preface and a postscript to his new book, *The Age of Reason*. He dedicated it, "To My Fellow Citizens of the United States," and in the preface said: "I have always strenuously supported the right of every man of his opinion, however different that opinion

THE

AGE OF REASON:

BEING AN INVESTIGATION OF

TRUE AND FABULOUS

THEOLOGY.

BY

THOMAS PAINE,

SECRETARY FOR FOREIGN AFFAIRS TO CONGRESS

IN THE AMERICAN WAR;

AND AUTHOR OF THE WORKS ENTITLED

COMMON SENSE, AND RIGHTS OF MAN,
&c. &c.

PARIS : PRINTED BY BARROIS.
1794.
[SECOND YEAR OF THE FRENCH REPUBLIC.]

Title page of The Age of Reason, *1794, published while
Paine was still in prison. It was the most controversial
of all his works.*

might be to mine. He who denies another this right, makes
a slave of himself to his present opinion, because he pre-
cludes himself the right of changing it."

His hopes rose when he learned from the prison
grapevine that two other Americans had been freed soon
after Americans living in Paris had petitioned the National
Convention. However, he could expect no help from
Gouverneur Morris, now the U.S. minister to France.

Morris, a champion of aristocracy who had supported royalty and deplored democratic rule, had no love for France. He hoped to end the treaty between France and the United States and to establish close ties with England instead. He and President Washington both believed America would benefit more from friendship with England than with revolutionary France. As for Paine, Morris had shown his contempt for the radical during their years in Philadelphia. He believed if an American got into trouble while living abroad, he had no right to seek help from his own country. That view, unfortunately, was confirmed later by President Washington.

If Morris would not help him, maybe his old friend Joel Barlow would. The Connecticut writer, now living in Paris, got permission for a delegation of Americans to speak for Paine in the convention. It was an eloquent plea, promising that if released, the "friend of humanity" would leave at once for America.

The plea was met with hisses. In icy tones the convention's president insisted that Paine was an Englishman, from a country at war with France, and therefore was an enemy of the Revolution. Frightened by this cold rejection, Paine wrote Morris that though they were "not on the best terms of harmony," he hoped Morris would inform the U.S. Congress of his plight and pressure the French to release him.

Nothing from Morris. Suddenly the police cut off all communication between Paine and the outside world. Yet whispers of the appalling events beyond the walls seeped through to him. More and more victims of the Terror were being arrested, grilled, executed. Even those within the topmost circle of power were now accused and murdered. Danton himself, revered as "the giant of the revolution," was charged with treason, thrown into prison, and executed.

Paine ticked off each day he survived as a blessing. "The state of things in the prison was a continued scene of horror," he recalled. "No one could count upon life for 24 hours. Scarcely a night passed in which ten, twenty, thirty, forty, fifty or more were taken out of the prison, carried before a pretended tribunal in the morning, and guillotined before night."

Yet somehow he achieved an inner serenity in the face of death. A prison friend who survived remembered Paine in those awful days:

> *His cheerful philosophy under the certain*
> *expectation of death, his sensibility of*
> *heart, his brilliant powers of conversation,*
> *and his sportive vein of wit rendered him*
> *a very general favorite with his compan-*
> *ions of misfortune, who found a refuge*
> *from evil in the charms of his society. He*
> *was the confidant of the unhappy, the*
> *counselor of the perplexed; and to his sym-*
> *pathizing friendship many a devoted vic-*
> *tim in the hour of death confided the last*
> *cares of humanity, and the last wishes of*
> *tenderness.*

At night, Paine continued to write in the glow of his candle. It was his way of not giving in, of showing defiance. He wrote two essays (that have been lost) and revised his *Rights of Man*, adding a new preface, and managed to have it smuggled out of prison.

Then, in June, prison life was made unimaginably worse. Cold, wet weather made his cell always damp, the prison's supply of fuel ran out, and there were no more candles to write by. Outside, a new revolutionary law did away with the wisps of judicial procedure. Prison rules were screwed tight. In one night alone 161 prisoners were wrenched from their cells and dragged off to the guillotine. Every night, Paine lay down on his straw in fear of never seeing his friends or the world again.

At the end of June, after six months in prison, Paine suddenly broke. Under the enormous weight of confinement and fear, he sank into a semiconsciousness that lasted for weeks. He was moved into a larger cell, shared with three Belgians. They did their best to keep him alive, feeding him, cleaning him, nursing him. Still, he did not get better, and they felt sure he would die. He could not eat, or talk, or gesture, or sit up. He had thinned to a skeleton, his skin turned dead white.

Then, on July 24, his number came up in the lottery of death. His name on the prison list was underscored in red by the public prosecutor. It signified execution within twenty-four hours. The next day, at six in the morning, a jailer with the death list walked the prison corridors, chalking a number on the outside of the cell doors of those to be carted away that night. When he came to Paine's cell, he chalked the number four on the inside of the door, for the door, which swung outward, was now open. The Belgians had secured permission to leave their door open during the day, so that whatever breeze coming through might cool Paine's fevered body.

A prison guard summons the condemned out of their cell to be taken to the guillotine for execution. It was only by a fluke that Paine escaped that fate.

When the death squad made their rounds that evening to collect the doomed, they passed by Paine's cell, for now the door was closed: they could not see the chalked number on the inside. That chance occurrence saved Paine's life.

A few days later, the Jacobin leader, Robespierre, fell from power and lost his head by the same guillotine that had killed thousands on his orders.

Again, hope. Maybe this meant Paine would be freed? As soon as he regained some strength, he wrote to the convention, pleading for his release. He pointed out that he was a citizen of the United States, France's ally, and that to call him a foreign enemy was a lie that only a Robespierre could invent.

Silence from the convention. Then luck seemed to go Paine's way, Gouverneur Morris was replaced as the U.S. minister to France by James Monroe, already living in Paris. Paine wrote Monroe three times that he could not be released without Monroe's help. Monroe did not reply because he was awaiting orders from the U.S. Congress. It still viewed Paine as a French citizen subject to that government's laws.

In desperation Paine wrote another letter to Monroe, forty-three pages long, arguing in great detail the case for his claim to U.S. citizenship and his rights under U.S. law.

At last, on September 18, Monroe responded. Yes, he wrote, you do have a right to U.S. citizenship and to my help: "By being with us through the revolution you are of our country, as absolutely as if you had been born there; and you are no more of England, then every native of America is." Monroe added that Paine's fellow Americans considered him "not only as having rendered important services in our own revolution, but as being, on a more extensive scale, the friend of human rights, and a distinguished and able advocate, in favor of the public liberty."

Nice words; but there was still no decisive action. More letters were exchanged, between Paine and Monroe and between Monroe and the French government. Then, on November 6, 1794, more than ten months since his arrest,

Paine's release was ordered. Monroe came to the Luxembourg that afternoon, and brought Paine to his own home, inviting him to be his guest indefinitely. To Monroe, twenty years younger, Paine was a hero of the American Revolution (in which Monroe had fought), to be treated with affection.

A month after his release, the convention reinstated Paine as a deputy, hailing him as "the cherished colleague of all the friends of man." Using what influence he had, Paine did his best to help those in need. He appealed for the release from prison of Lafayette's wife and children (Lafayette himself was in prison in Austria) and helped friends get passports from the Foreign Office.

Again, he stepped into politics. The convention was about to decide on still another constitution, and he wanted to help write it. He felt, more strongly than ever, that France needed a written constitution based on the rights of man:

> Had a constitution been established, the nation would then have had a bond of union, and every individual would have known the line of conduct he was to follow. But instead of this, a revolutionary government, a thing without either principle or authority, was substitute in its place; virtue and crime depended upon accident; and that which was patriotism one day became treason the next.

Those who had opposed the Jacobins played the major role in the writing of the new constitution. The draft dropped the principle of universal suffrage. As a French aristocrat put it, "We should be governed by the best...the most educated and the most interested in maintaining the laws." By that he meant only property owners were fit to govern. Under the new constitution, to vote or hold office you had to be a man of property. Those with a more democratic view were so discouraged they put up little resistance to this rightward turn.

It was Paine, standing almost alone, who criticized the new constitution and reaffirmed the principle of universal suffrage. (Which meant, at that time, all men but not women.) On July 7 he appeared in the convention hall for the first time in two years, to deliver his views on the new constitution. He stood by silently on the tribune as someone read the French translation of his speech. He argued that he himself had no objection to property, so long as it was not criminally gained or criminally used. But to make it the condition for the right to vote was dangerous, ridiculous, and unjust. It would deny the vote to half the population. In reacting against the Terror, he went on, "don't subvert the basis of the Revolution. If you dispense with principles and substitute expedients, you will extinguish that enthusiasm and energy which have hitherto been the life and soul of the Revolution; and you will substitute in its place nothing but cold self-interest."

When the speech was over, no one stood to praise it. His appeal was ignored. With the draft completed, the constitution was sent to the people and ratified by them. A new government was elected, one Paine had no faith in. It was the end of his service as a legislator.

❖ 19 ❖

THE AGE OF
REASON

*I believe in one God, and no more, and I hope
to find happiness beyond this life.... I believe in
the equality of men, and I believe, that religious duties consist in doing justice, having
mercy, and endeavoring to make our fellow-
creatures happy.*

—Thomas Paine

When Paine was arrested in December, 1793, he
had the manuscript of the first part of *The Age of
Reason* with him. The police let him send it to his
friend Joel Barlow, for safekeeping. Barlow had it published while Paine was still in prison. It was a small book,
only fifty-five pages.

By the time Paine got out, *The Age of Reason* had stirred
even more controversy than his earlier pamphlets had.
Strangely, while he wrote it to combat what he saw as the
growth of atheism in France, it has often been taken as a
defense of atheism. He was called a blackguard (unscrupu-
lous person) for his attack upon organized religion. Others
said that though they liked the work, "It is better not to dis-
turb the devout mind by fanciful and newfangled schemes
of belief which should be open only to the eyes of the
learned." Criticism of Part I came mostly from clergymen.
Paine replied that each claimed to understand the Bible
best, "though each understands it differently," and that

"they agreed on nothing but in telling their readers that Thomas Paine understands it not."

While writing Part I of the work, Paine had worked under difficult conditions, with no Bible handy. Now, in the Monroe home, with a Bible beside him, he produced a far more detailed analysis of it.

Published in October 1, 1795, Part II ran more than half again the length of Part I. He was so confident of large sales that he had the printer run off fifteen thousand copies for the American market alone. He paid for it probably with a loan from Monroe, from whom he often borrowed money.

What is in *The Age of Reason*? And why did he write it?

During the early 1790s, Paine observed that the accelerating Jacobin attack on religion was pushing the people of France "headlong into atheism." He was convinced something needed to be done to arrest that movement. He said he wrote *The Age of Reason* because now that France had abolished the priesthood completely, there was danger that "in the general wreck of superstition, of false systems of government and false theology, we lose sight of morality, of humanity, and of the theology that is true."

That was his aim. Yet it was this work that would falsely label him as an atheist, the enemy of all religion. For Paine was by no means an atheist. It was not God but churches and religious institutions he regarded as "engines of power" and devices attempting "to terrify and enslave mankind, and monopolize power and profit."

Long before, first in England and then in America, Paine had told friends that he would like to put down on paper his ideas on religion. Maybe not now, but in "the latter part of my life." He had been raised in a Quaker-Anglican family, and later had absorbed some of Methodism. Then, attracted by Newtonian science, he had come to detest what he called "superstition" and "imposture" in religious practices. During the American Revolution he had endorsed the separation of church and state and freedom of expression for all faiths.

On his return to England, he was shocked to hear politicians and preachers explain away poverty by saying it is the will of God that there be poor people. And did not those oppressors—King George and all monarchs—claim their thrones as their divine right?

In France, he found that the people were not opposed to religion itself but to the way the Church had become a pillar of the feudal system. As the Revolution gained more strength, the Church became identified with the counter-revolution, and all sorts of restrictions were placed upon it.

So in writing *The Age of Reason*, Paine set out to disarm the power of organized religion. What he had to say was not at all new. Many others had said it before him. It was his eloquence that made his work so striking. The basic tenets of Christianity—revelation, miracles, the divine inspiration of the Bible—did not stand up to reason, he argued. The true source of spirituality is not the Bible and revelation, he said, but nature and natural laws: "The word of God is the creation we behold, and it is in this word, which no human intervention can counter or alter, that

The young artist John Wesley Jarvis befriended Paine in his last down-and-out years and painted this portrait of him.

God speaketh universally to man." He saw the power of God in "the immensity of the creation," and divine wisdom in "the unchangeable order of the universe." Witness to God's benevolence was "the abundance" with which he fills the earth.

These were the beliefs of people called Deists, like Washington, Jefferson, and Franklin. But they had cherished Deism quietly, in private. They had not broadcast it to the people. Many men and women in the seventeenth and eighteenth centuries held deistic views. Though they varied on some points, all agreed in trying to construct a natural religion by reason alone. In more modern times people who have seen religion in this light have been called freethinkers.

In Paine's time, most Deists voiced their religious opinions in their own upper-class circles or wrote for an educated readership. But Paine, as in all his work, aimed at a much larger mass audience. His book saw print in a great many editions and languages, winning a place as the most popular deistic work ever written. What appalled Church leaders was that disturbing ideas once confined to a tiny minority, the elite, were now reaching a mass audience. And with a vivid, aggressive, antichurch tone. The results, said historian Eric Foner, was that *The Age of Reason* "helped shake men free from deference to religious institutions, just as Paine's other writing led his readers to rethink their assumptions about politics and society."

Paine's language was harsh. He often sounded like the militant Jacobins who called religion nothing but "superstition and fanaticism." Yet he opposed their program of using force to uproot religious belief. He thought Jacobins went much too far in their dechristianization program, crushing the civility and personal freedom vital to democracy. Atheism is antidemocratic, he said. To destroy religion would destroy morality, compassion, love. And replace them with unbridled self-interest, egoism, lies, and vicious struggles for power.

Yet Paine's view of religion and the Church was narrowly limited. He denied that the Bible was literally true, but he was blind to its metaphoric and mythic qualities. As for the Church, yes, in France and other parts of Europe it was the bulwark of despotic power and enjoyed special privileges. Still, Paine ignored the many independent, voluntary congregations of believers. And the power of religious revivals to set free great reform movements. That is why *The Age of Reason* angered dissenters of many kinds, who refused to reject Christianity and the Bible. So while

An example of the propaganda against Paine, calling him all sorts of bad names, sponsored by the British government in the 1790s.

Paine aided the secular radical movements, he cut himself off from the religious reformers.

In England, the government decided to label *The Age of Reason* blasphemous, and in 1797 sentenced one man to a year of hard labor for selling the work. Nevertheless, thousands of copies of a cheap edition circulated, even reaching underground to the miners at Cornwall.

In America, eight editions appeared in 1794, seven the following year, and two in 1796. Thousands of copies were sold to Philadelphians for a mere one and a half cents each. This alarmed the clergy because even "children, servants and the lowest people" were tempted to buy it. At Yale, Harvard, and Dartmouth the work became so popular that the authorities felt compelled to hand students a refutation of Paine's argument.

When he finished Part II, Paine began a brief vacation but fell so sick he had to return to the Monroes. They were so anxious about him that they canceled their own plans for a vacation and took on nursing him back to health. He became as helpless as a very sick child. Monroe thought Paine would die within a month. Paine himself did not expect to live much longer. In this gloomy state of mind he began to express bitterness toward George Washington. In a letter to James Madison he said, "I owe this illness (from which I have not much prospect of recovering) partly to Robespierre and partly to Mr. Washington." Why hadn't the president done anything to get him out of prison? "I ought not to have suspected Mr. Washington of treachery but he has acted towards me the part of a cold-blooded traitor."

Later, in 1796, Paine published an open "Letter to George Washington." It was a harsh condemnation, calling Washington "the patron of fraud... treacherous in private friendship... and a hypocrite in public life." The world, he said, would be "puzzled to decide, whether you are an apostate or an imposter, whether you have abandoned good principles, or whether you ever had any." It was hard to believe this came from Paine, a man who had been Washington's warm friend and ardent supporter.

Perhaps there are excuses for it. Paine had just gone through a terrible ordeal in prison and had not yet recovered his health. He could not understand why Washington could be so indifferent to a friend's fate, to one who had dedicated *The Rights of Man* to him. Even if the president had been deceived by Gouverneur Morris, he should have investigated Paine's case for himself.

But there was another cause for anger behind the letter. The president, Paine believed, had aligned himself with the new Federalist party—the conservatives who were seeking to restore good relations with George III and scheming to turn America into a monarchy.

Paine even went so far as to forget his frequent praise of Washington's military skill during the Revolution. Now he said Washington had been overrated as a general, had been so inept he had almost lost the war. If not for French aid, the Americans would not have beaten Britain. And yet Washington was now abandoning France while opening his arms to England.

Paine was unable to see what had happened to him from Washington's perspective. Sometimes a president's personal wishes conflict with his duty to the government. He had to keep American interests uppermost, not the private concerns of an individual.

That public letter to Washington did great damage to Paine and to his friends, the Jeffersonians. It delighted Paine's enemies, conservatives who had always hated the radical. And now here was the author of the scandalous *Age of Reason* daring to denounce the president of the United States. These same people, leading the new Federalist party, used the letter as well as *The Age of Reason* as weapons against the Jeffersonians and their Republican party.

With the anger out of his system and his health restored, Paine turned to a new issue—social and economic welfare.

❖ 20 ❖

A PLEA FOR SOCIAL JUSTICE

Nothing angered Paine more than the gross contrast between the lives of the rich and the poor. Always ready to spring to the defense of the poor, in the winter of 1795–96, while living with the Monroes, he wrote a powerful pamphlet on the relation of government to social well-being. Called *Agrarian Justice*, it was published a year later. In it he said:

> *The present state of civilization is as odious as it is unjust. It is absolutely the opposite of what it should be, and it is necessary that a revolution should be made in it. The contrast of affluence and wretchedness continually meeting and offending the eye is like dead and living bodies chained together.... The great mass of the poor are becoming an hereditary race, and it is next to impossible for them to get out of that state of themselves.... The condition of millions, in every country in Europe, is far worse than if they had been born before civilization began.*

Paine himself had often suffered poverty in the past, and would again in the future. He knew intimately what that life was like. In his England, the vast majority of the population were classed as "the laboring poor." The brutal enclosure movement of the last half of the eighteenth century was driving huge numbers of peasants off the land and into the rising industrial centers. But the change did little to improve their lot. The life of most of the working poor was almost unbearable. "Hours were intolerably long, wages low, housing unsanitary and hunger commonplace," wrote historian J. H. Plumb.

The question Paine considered in his new pamphlet is still at the heart of our social problems. Is civilization able

Shopkeepers, tradesmen, and mechanics, influenced by Paine's writings, formed the London Corresponding Society to fight against inequality of wealth and liberties. This anti-radical caricature of 1798 ridicules the members. Note the picture of Paine on the back wall.

to cure the disease of poverty that it spreads everywhere?

Only a handful of people felt the problem of poverty could be solved. Most of the upper class, in the words of the Bishop of Llandaff, believed in "the wisdom and goodness of God, in having made both rich and poor."

Paine wrote his pamphlet partly in reply to the views expressed in the bishop's sermon and partly to sound the alarm over what the conservatives in France were doing. Having overthrown the Jacobins, they were trying to restore property and privilege to the upper classes.

"It is wrong," Paine said, "to say God made rich and poor. He made only male and female; and He gave them the earth for their inheritance." Poverty did not exist in humankind's natural state, and neither did property. A landlord properly owns only the improvements he makes on a piece of land, not the land itself.

Paine did not ask that property be divided up and parceled out equally to all. He asked only that those people who had lost their land to the monopolizers—lost their share of the common inheritance of the earth, as he put it— should be paid an indemnity. A ten-percent inheritance tax would accomplish that. It would correct an unjust system without harming the present occupants of the land, whom Paine considered innocent. That tax money would provide a national fund for the endowment of the young and the pensioning of the old. It was an early proposal for the idea of social security, expanding on some of the measures offered in *The Rights of Man*, but more radical in nature.

Notice how the land and what should be done with it figures so powerfully in *Agrarian Justice*, even in its title. That is because Paine's vision was shaped in a society still deeply rooted in the land. His thinking on this issue was in many respects like that of others, including Thomas Jefferson. At its core was the belief that because "the earth, in its natural uncultivated state, was, and ever would have continued to be, the common property of the human race," society owed every person a livelihood—not as a matter of charity but of justice.

Paine made another point, about the source of wealth:

"The accumulation of personal property is, in many instances, the effect of paying too little for the labor that produced it; and the consequence of which is that the working hand perishes in old age, and the employer abounds in affluence."

Paine's ideas on this issue were in conflict with what others thought. He believed with many Enlightenment thinkers that there was nothing sacred about private property. It was a social arrangement limited by social needs. And it could be altered democratically by a majority of the people. Others held that private property was an absolute right—beyond the reach of any government's action.

Clearly, in his later years, Paine's great concern was for the well-being of society. He wanted to eliminate poverty, not the system of private property. Call him liberal or progressive; he was not a socialist. To achieve a more just social system, he believed that popular control of government was an essential preliminary. He expected nothing from the old order of monarchs and aristocrats.

Paine absorbed ideas like a sponge and worked them out in pamphlets that reshaped the way millions looked at their world. With an original mind—a rare gift!—he looked at the life around him through his own eyes. He put it beautifully early on, when he said: "When precedents fail to assist us, we must return to the first principles of things for information, and think as if we were the first men that thought."

Even though Paine was unhappy with the reaction that set in, he remained in France until 1802. Under the third constitution an elaborate structure of checks and balances was established, to guarantee order after the bloody chaos of previous years. Executive power was handed to a Directory of five men. However, there was no procedure to handle a deadlock between the legislative and executive branches, which made the seizure of power in a coup quite likely.

The Directory lasted four years. During that time there was a brief peace between France and other nations, except for England. It turned out to be only a truce, and war began again on an even larger scale than before. It was the proving ground for the spectacular rise of a young revolutionary general, Napoléon Bonaparte. In 1799 he seized power, ending the Directory. For the next two decades, his career would dominate the history of Europe.

In the spring of 1797, Paine, now 60, left the Monroe home and moved in with the family of Nicolas de Bonneville. It was supposed to be temporary, but he stayed more than five years. Paine had become Bonneville's friend several years earlier. Bonneville had edited various political journals and published the French translation of *The Age of Reason*, and many of Paine's other writings. Now Bonneville provided Paine with a bedroom and a study, "my workshop," Paine called it. His old customs revived: reading the newspapers daily, writing, chatting with visitors, napping after lunch, taking long walks afterwards. One of his visitors was Wolfe Tone, the Irish Republican living in Paris. In his diary Tone reported Paine was a great talker and a witty fellow, but "he drinks like a fish, a misfortune which I have seen befall other celebrated patriots."

Despite the twists and turns of the Revolution, Paine admired France for ending feudalism and autocracy. He still hoped democracy, however troubled its course, would one day develop to the full a society benefiting all humankind. He supported especially France's war with England, the country he believed was the bulwark of reaction in Europe. If England could be defeated, the aristocracy would collapse. The way would be open to a democratic republic. And joining together with France and the United States, England could assure the spread of democratic government throughout the world. "There will be no lasting peace for France, nor for the world," Paine wrote, "until the tyranny and corruption of the English government be abolished, and England...become a sister republic."

While living with the Bonnevilles, Paine paid no rent, for he had little income. In return he offered to have the Bonnevilles come live with him in the United States whenever they wished. It looked like the Bonnevilles would need shelter, for in 1799 the police had suppressed Bonneville's paper for its frequent criticism of Napoléon. That blow just about bankrupted the editor, who had never been rich.

As France moved on the path toward dictatorship, Paine seemed blind to the eventual outcome. He found excuses for the step-by-step loss of liberty, insisting these were temporary measures to prevent the restoration of monarchy. He constantly drew parallels between the American Revolution and the developments in France, expecting the French Revolution would turn out as well.

His pieces on foreign affairs were translated by Mme Bonneville and printed in her husband's paper. Paine no longer believed that right would always conquer might, that armies were not needed to accomplish that. Now he argued that sometimes it took military power to convert principles into reality. He followed closely the French campaigns in Europe, rejoicing at the defeat of autocracy in country after country. Paine began to dream of a French invasion of England that would spark a glorious uprising of English, Welsh, and Scottish commoners. In 1797 he urged Napoléon to do it, working out a detailed plan for it. Napoléon liked the proposal so much that he invited Paine to dinner to talk it over. The general thought Paine should accompany the invasion forces as a political adviser and then join a provisional English revolutionary government. He declared that every city in the world should erect a golden statue of Paine, adding that he always slept with a copy of *The Rights of Man* under his pillow.

Despite the flattery, which Paine loved, no invasion ever took place. And the compliments turned into insults. Meeting Paine again much later, Napoléon, while staring right at Paine, said loudly to an officer next him, "The English are all alike; in every country they are rascals."

Friends reported that Paine began to call Napoléon "willful, headstrong, proud," a tyrant "who committed so many faults and crimes" with so little reason. He was careful in his criticism of Napoléon's regime, confining it to private letters and conversations. He gave up "all hopes that any good will be done by France—that honor is reserved for America."

Late in 1800 he was immensely heartened when he learned that the conservative Federalist party of President John Adams had been defeated and that his old friend Thomas Jefferson had been elected the third president of the United States.

Soon after Jefferson took office, he wrote Paine inviting him to return to the United States. You can sail on one of our warships, he said, as the honored guest of the nation you helped to create. You'll find a warm welcome now, for this administration is not like its predecessors. And he concluded, "That you may live long to continue your useful labors, and to reap your reward in the thankfulness of nations, is my sincere prayer. Accept assurances of my high esteem and affectionate attachment."

But it was more than a year before Paine left. On September 1, 1802, he boarded a ship at Le Havre, bound for Baltimore. He would never see Europe again.

❖ 21 ❖

UNHAPPY ENDING

When Paine landed at Baltimore on October 30, 1802, he was greeted at the wharf by a crowd of excited Jeffersonians. They took him off to a nearby tavern where he displayed models of his bridge that he had brought with him. He made a short speech and answered questions about his years abroad. One reporter described him as "decently clad," with short gray hair and a long, drooping red nose.

His pleasure in returning to America lasted scarcely a day. Attacks upon him by political enemies that had begun while he was still abroad multiplied when he came in sight. Both *The Age of Reason* and his "Letter to George Washington" enraged the conservatives. Editorials called him "loathsome reptile," "demi-human arch-beast," "lying, drunken, brutal infidel," "object of disgust, of abhorrence, of absolute loathing to every decent man except the President of the United States."

When he looked for comfort to friends of revolutionary days, he found doors closed to him. Samuel Adams broke away, and Benjamin Rush refused to have anything to do with him. Both said they found his ideas on religion too "offensive."

Soon Paine settled in at Lovell's, the only hotel in Washington, the new capital city—or village really, for much of it was still undeveloped swampland, and the Capitol and the White House had yet to be completed. Charge and countercharge volleyed in the press as the Republicans and Federalists struggled to keep or regain power. Paine plunged into party politics with a series of letters in the *National Intelligencer*, edited by an English political exile who had once been prosecuted back home for his support of Paine.

Paine's article warned of the sorry effects of violent partisanship that he had observed in France, where fierce words had led to executions. But he believed Americans would "think for themselves, and judge of government, not by the fury of newspaper writers, but by the prudent frugality of its measures, and the encouragement it gives to the improvement and prosperity of the country."

Watching Paine for some weeks as he moved about Washington, the friendly correspondent of a Worcester newspaper, the *National Aegis*, wrote:

> *Years have made more impression on his body than his mind. He bends a little forward, carries one hand in the other behind, when he walks. He dresses plain like a farmer, and appears cleanly and comfortably in person, unless in the article of snuff which he uses in profusion. His address is unaffected and unceremonious. He neither shuns nor courts observation. At table he enjoys what is good, with the appetite of temperance and vigor, and puts to shame his calumniators, by the moderation with which he partakes of the common beverage of the boarders. His conversation is uncommonly interesting; he is gay, humorous, and full of anecdote—his memory preserves its full capacity, and his mind is irresistible.*

To rumors that he sought patronage from his friend Jefferson, Paine replied he had no interest in a government job. His only aim was to do what he had long done—be a political writer serving the public interest. The unrelenting attacks upon Paine did not scare off the president. Jefferson invited Paine many times to come talk with him. Paine dined at the executive mansion, and the two men were seen out walking together, arm in arm.

Members of the cabinet, too, had Paine in for dinner. His extraordinary personal history and his lively conversation, rich in stories of the wars and revolutions he had been part of, made him an entertaining guest. Jefferson's intimacy with Paine did not escape criticism, of course. The mildest word Federalist editors had for it was "nauseating." Although the publicly displayed friendship did him no good, Jefferson remained loyal to Paine.

Paine had a hand in the major triumph of Jefferson's first term—the purchase of the Louisiana Territory. Knowing Napoléon's treasury was almost broke, with cash desperately needed, Paine was one of the first to suggest to Jefferson that the United States buy not only the port of New Orleans, the original intention, but the entire vast Louisiana Territory. In May 1803, the French ceded the territory to the United States for a total price of fifteen million dollars. That act removed the French from competition on this continent and doubled the size of the American

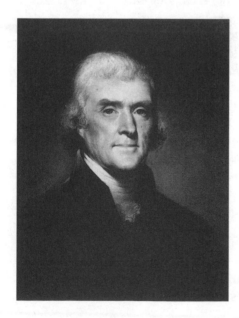

Thomas Jefferson, painted by Rembrandt Peale in 1800. Paine's suggestion to the president helped bring about the Louisiana Purchase of 1803.

empire. Paine then suggested to Jefferson how the new lands might be incorporated into the Union.

When the French living in Louisiana asked the U.S. Congress to grant their territory statehood, they wanted to be allowed to continue slavery and the slave trade. Paine wrote a public letter to them, pointing out how contradictory it was that those who had achieved freedom would now deprive another people of that freedom.

Leaving Washington on his way to New York, Paine stopped in Philadelphia. Only a few old friends wanted to see him, among them Charles Willson Peale, the eminent portrait painter who had just moved his museum into Independence Hall. Collecting everything from Native American artifacts to dinosaur bones, he offered to add Paine's bridge models to the museum's collection.

A few days later Paine was in New Jersey, where he was reunited with Mme. Bonneville and her three boys, one of them named for him. Paine had paid their passage to America, as he had promised. At Trenton, two stage-coach drivers refused passage to New York for "this infidel," and when a third driver seated him, a mob gathered to throw stones. Paine calmly faced them down, and the frightened horse pulled off.

Happily for Paine New York was different. Strangers came up to him to shake his hand and welcome him back. The city was full of immigrants from Britain, who hailed him on the street to say they had read *The Rights of Man* and to offer their best wishes to "the man whose writings have made so much noise in the world," as one man put it.

As the winter of 1803–4 came on, Paine decided to spend it quietly at his farm in New Rochelle. He arrived before the first snow fell, but an acutely painful attack of gout, a rheumatic disease that produces severe inflammation, laid him low. Suddenly he could do nothing. Walking, sleeping, working were all difficult or impossible. A local store clerk took him in for nursing until he recovered two months later.

In March he retreated from the harsh winter to New York City. There he and the Bonnevilles took rooms in a

Paine lived in this house on 293 Bleecker Street in Greenwich Village in 1808–09.

boarding house. Stronger now, he walked the streets and made the rounds of dinner parties. He began to write again, this time several public letters on his views of religion for a journal edited by Elihu Palmer, a Deist like himself. Many of the pieces compared the various world religions, almost as an anthropologist would. He concluded that "the belief of a God is a universal article common to all religions," and that the power to reason—to live in truth—was God's gift to all humanity.

Palmer, a former Methodist, believed Paine was "the undaunted champion of reason, and the resolute enemy of tyranny, bigotry and prejudice...probably the most useful man that ever existed on the face of the earth."

In the fall Paine was back in New Rochelle. Now sixty-seven, a very old age in his day, he sank into a dismal life of near poverty. Unable to keep his accounts, he ran up debts that forced him to sell off sixty of his acres. The sale netted enough to leave him with something to pay an African-American woman who came in to cook his meals, wash his clothes, and try to clean up the mess he lived in. He kept himself to one small room, like a hermit, said a visitor who guessed all the furniture he had wasn't worth five dollars.

Still, he made plans to enlarge his cottage, describing them to Jefferson, a distinguished architect in addition to his many other talents. In his reply the president pointed out some problems with the design. More financial pressure, however, forced Paine to drop the project.

Once again he returned to New York for the winter, to stay in the home of William Carver, a blacksmith and veterinarian, whom Paine had known back in Lewes. In the spring, Paine made plans to publish his complete writings in six volumes, to be paid for upon delivery to subscribers. He thought his work would help future generations to remember their revolutionary heritage. The task proved too difficult for a man whose energy was almost gone. In his few remaining years he was able only to write letters and a dozen or so articles on political issues that could still excite him.

He went downhill rapidly. Miserable and depressed, he feared that America had forgotten him. He refused to let his housekeeper do anything for him, ate almost nothing, drank a lot, and seemed bent on destroying himself. His friend Carver drove up from New York to see him and was appalled to find Paine ragged and filthy, smelling like "our poor beggars in England." He bathed Paine, sobered him up, provided clean clothing, and bundled him into his buggy to drive him to his home in New York.

That change saved Paine from imminent death. Life with his generous friend revived him. Through the Carvers he met many working people who treated him respectfully as "a friend of the people" who had made great gifts to them through his writings. He regained strength enough to write an essay on the acute infectious disease yellow fever, which regularly devastated whole communities, especially in southern states. He surmised it was not a domestic but an imported infection. Later, investigators confirmed his theory, finding that mosquitoes carried the disease aboard ships sailing from the Caribbean to the eastern seaboard states. Paine's essay was widely reprinted in several states, especially in the South.

His pleasure in the praise he earned was cut short when one evening at the Carvers he suffered a stroke as he climbed the stairs to bed. Unconscious, he fell in a heap to the bottom of the stairs. Although he recovered after many months, his demands upon the Carvers proved too much, and the friendship turned sour. He began to drink heavily again and was asked to leave.

Now he would move from place to place, living with this person or that for brief periods. He continued to write Congress, asking for the grant of a tract of land, which he could sell. He believed the government owed it to him for his services in the American Revolution. No answer. His last letter to Jefferson asked the president to intervene with Congress. Jefferson replied he was afraid it would do no good. Finally Congress confirmed the refusal in a formal letter to Paine.

In 1808, Paine was in such bad condition that friends moved him into a room in what is now Greenwich Village in New York City. To pay the expenses he had to sell his small property in Bordentown. Sensing death was near, he drew up his will, leaving small sums to various people who had helped him, the largest bequest going to Mme. Bonneville, to support and educate her sons. He hoped he would be buried in Quaker ground, if the Quakers would permit it. And in closing the will, he said: "I have lived an honest and useful life to mankind; my time has been spent in doing good, and I die in perfect composure and resignation to the will of my Creator, God."

The Quakers refused his request, bringing him to tears. Mme. Bonneville, who visited him regularly in these last months, assured him she would arrange for him to be buried on his farm in New Rochelle. Hearing that Paine was dying, former friends like the Carvers came to comfort him. As he became too weak to talk, he asked that someone always be in the room with him. He did not want to die alone.

Around nine in the morning on June 8, 1809, he died peacefully in his sleep. He was seventy-two years old.

Few people were present when Paine was buried in a corner of his field near a roadside. Only a handful of his

The English periodical The British Workman *published this sketch by John Gilbert called* The Last Moments of Paine.

New Rochelle neighbors attended—a Quaker and two African-Americans. Almost no newspaper noticed his death. No dignitaries came to speak of Paine's life and its meaning. The apprentice from Thetford was buried as though he had never accomplished anything in this world.

Among those beside the grave were Mme. Bonneville and two of her sons. Later she wrote:

> *This interment was a scene to affect and to wound any sensible heart. Contemplating who it was, what man it was, that we were committing to an obscure grave on an open and disregarded bit of land, I could not help feeling most acutely. Before the earth was thrown down upon the coffin, I, placing myself at the east end of the grave, said to my son Benjamin, "stand you there, at the other end, as a witness for grateful America." Looking round me, and beholding the small group of spectators, I exclaimed as the earth was tumbled into the grave, "Oh! Mr. Paine! My son stands here as testimony of the gratitude of America, and I, for France!" This was the funeral ceremony of this great politician and philosopher!*

❖ AFTERWORD ❖

Almost no one seemed to care about Tom Paine for some years after his death. In 1819 his farm house in New Rochelle burned down and that same year William Cobbett, an English radical who had emigrated to America, dug up Paine's bones and carried them back to England. He exhibited them at Liverpool, hoping to raise enough money for a monument to "the common sense of the great man." But when he failed, the box of bones passed from hand to hand until it disappeared.

In 1839, a monument to Paine was erected in New Rochelle, the town which in 1807 had denied him the right to vote in the local elections on the ground that he was not a citizen. The monument was restored and rededicated in 1881, and a bronze bust was unveiled in 1887. Not until 1945, however, did the town restore his citizenship. Independence Hall in Philadelphia honored Paine for his great role in the American Revolution by accepting a portrait of him in 1875 and a bronze bust in 1905. On January 29, 1968, the United States issued a postage stamp to commemorate Paine's birthday.

In 1992, an act of Congress approved erecting a monument to Paine in the District of Columbia. In 1994, the National Capital Memorial Commission voted unanimously to authorize a memorial to Paine on the Mall, where so many great figures of the past are honored.

In England, Paine was honored in 1964 with a statue erected in Thetford, his birthplace. (Paine holds a quill pen in his right hand and a copy of *The Rights of Man* in his left hand.) In 1987, on the 250th anniversary of Paine's birth, the Thomas Paine Society of England sponsored meetings and exhibits in several towns and cities, including Thetford. The anniversary was marked in the United

States, too, and funds were raised to modernize and expand the Thomas Paine Memorial Museum in New Rochelle. Ironically, President Ronald Reagan, whose beliefs were far removed from Paine's, saw fit in 1984 to pay tribute to him, citing the line, "These are the times that try men's souls," and hailing Paine for the "invaluable contribution" of his *Crisis* papers.

But more important than monuments and museums are words, the words Paine wrote that shaped history. His own writings have been reprinted worldwide in innumerable editions, and the study of his amazingly productive life and work has drawn more and more scholars and biographers. Thanks to Tom Paine, debate over fundamental issues that had been the exclusive province of the upper class was invaded by the insistent voices of all sorts of people. The political theory that preached the static and eternal nature of society was replaced by Paine's proclamation of ceaseless change. The people who once had remained silent on the sidelines now demanded their place at the center. Paine helped people to see that a soldier was as good as an officer, a baker as good as a banker, a peasant as good as a landlord, and a commoner much better than a king.

Many generations of working men and women have read Paine's works and learned from him. It is important to note his specific ideas on politics and religion, but, more important, to understand the central thrust of his writings. He made people realize they had a right to look at life through their own eyes, to question long-accepted beliefs and practices, and to judge the world for themselves. In doing so, he inspired the self-confidence needed to challenge things as they are and to work together for a better world.

❖ NOTE ON SOURCES ❖

There is less material on Paine than on many of the other people who figured prominently in the American Revolution and the French Revolution. Despite his great contribution to both historical events, he never held a high office that would have produced a great stream of official papers. In addition to the best-known and most important of his works—*Common Sense*, *The Rights of Man*, and *The Age of Reason*—his writings consist mainly of private and public letters together with over six hundred pieces published as pamphlets or in newspapers and magazines.

The interest of biographers and historians in Paine goes back to his own lifetime and has led to many studies, a number that has grown rapidly in recent years. Scholarly monographs on various aspects of Paine's life and thought have also multiplied.

Only those works that are readily accessible are listed here. First there are the sources in his own words, then the biographies of Paine, and finally some of the works I relied on for historical background.

Readers who wish to go to Paine's own words will find several editions of his collected writings. The first to appear, edited by Philip S. Foner, was *The Life and Major Writings of Thomas Paine*, two volumes, Citadel, 1948. (Only the first volume is still in print.) It contains *Common Sense*, *The American Crisis* papers, *The Rights of Man*, *The Age of Reason*, and *Agrarian Justice*.

The same basic works, minus *Agrarian Justice*, are in *Thomas Paine: Political Writings*, Cambridge University Press, 1989, edited by Bruce Kuklick.

The Thomas Paine Reader, edited by Michael Foot and Isaac Kramnick, Penguin, 1987, has everything in the Foner volume one, plus sixteen other major pieces. It is not annotated.

Eric Foner, whose Paine biography is listed below, has edited and annotated the Library of America volume, *Thomas Paine: Collected Writings, 1995.*

There have been many biographies of Paine. The first, by the royalist George Chalmers, published in 1791, when Paine was in his fifties and living in London, was a scurrilous piece of hack work. The most recent biography is by John Keane, *Tom Paine: A Political Life*, Little, Brown, 1995. This is the most comprehensive, most thoroughly documented, and the best balanced of all I have read. Others I used are Jack Fruchtman, Jr., *Thomas Paine: Apostle of Freedom*, Four Walls, Eight Windows, 1994; David Freeman Hawke, *Paine*, Norton, 1974, and Eric Foner, *Tom Paine and Revolutionary America*, Oxford University Press, 1976. I also went back to the first solid biography, by Moncure Conway, an American abolitionist sympathetic to Paine. Called *The Life of Thomas Paine*, it appeared in two volumes in 1892 and was the product of intensive research. It retains its place as the first well-documented source all subsequent lives have drawn on. Hard to obtain now, I found it in the library of the New York Historical Society.

Among the many other books on Paine are some that offer close analysis of his ideas as expressed in his writings, with less space given to the narrative of his life. I used Alfred Owen Aldridge, *Man of Reason: The Life of Thomas Paine*, Lippincott, 1959; A. J. Ayer, *Thomas Paine*, Univ. of Chicago Press, 1988; Gregory Claes, *Thomas Paine: Social and Political Thought*, Unwin Hyman, 1989; and Mark Philp, *Paine*, Oxford University Press, 1989.

An excellent essay, "Thomas Paine, Republican Pamphleteer," appears in *Main Currents in American Thought*, volume 1, by Vernon L. Parrington, University of Oklahoma Press, 1987. A provocative study by David A. Wilson is *Paine and Cobbett: The Transatlantic Connection*, McGill-Queens, 1988. (Cobbett was an anti-Jacobin who converted to radicalism and reclaimed Paine's bones for England.)

SELECTED REFERENCE WORKS

Alden, John Richard. *The American Revolution: 1775-1783,* Harper, 1954.

Berlin, Isaiah. *The Crooked Timber of Humanity: Chapters in the History of Ideas.* Vintage, 1992.

Burlingame, Roger. *The American Conscience,* Knopf, 1957.

Countryman, Edward. *The American Revolution.* Hill & Wang, 1985.

Davidson, Philip. *Propaganda and the American Revolution, 1763-1783.* University of North Carolina Press, 1941.

Gipson, Laurence H. *The Coming of the American Revolution, 1763-1775.* Harper, 1954.

Goodwin, Albert. *The Friends of Liberty: The English Democratic Movement in the Age of the French Revolution.* Harvard University Press, 1979.

Green, Martin. *Prophets of a New Age: The Politics of Hope from the 18th Through the 20th Centuries.* Scribner's, 1992.

Greene, Jack P., ed. *The American Revolution: Its Character and Limits.* New York University Press, 1987.

Hudson, Frederick. *Journalism in America, 1690-1872.* Harper, 1872.

Lynd, Staughton. *Intellectual Origins of American Radicalism.* Pantheon, 1968.

Maier, Pauline. *The Old Revolutionaries.* Knopf, 1980.

—. *From Resistance to Revolution.* Vintage, 1974.

Miller, John C. *Origins of the American Revolution.* Little, Brown, 1943.

Miroff, Bruce. *Icons of Democracy.* Basic, 1993.

Morgan, Edmond S. *The Birth of the Republic, 1763-1789.* University of Chicago Press, 1956.

Morris, Richard B. *The Forging of the Union, 1781-1789.* Harper, 1960.

Nye, Russell B. *The Cultural Life of the New Nation, 1776-1830.* Harper, 1960.

Plumb, J. H. *England in the Eighteenth Century.* Penguin, 1990.

Rude, George. *Ideology and Popular Protest.* Pantheon, 1980.

Schama, Simon. *Citizens: A Chronicle of the French Revolution.* Knopf, 1989.

Tebbel, John. The Compact History of the American Newspaper. Hawthorne, 1963.

Thompson, E. P. *The Making of the English Working Class.* Vintage, 1966.

Wills, Garry. *Inventing America: Jefferson's Declaration of Independence.* Doubleday, 1978.

Wood, Gordon S. *The Radicalism of the American Revolution.* Knopf, 1992.

❖ INDEX ❖

❖ ABOUT THE AUTHOR ❖

Milton Meltzer has published more than ninety books for young people and adults in the fields of history, biography, and social issues and has also dealt with such diverse topics as the horse, gold, the potato, memory, and names. He has written and edited for newspapers, magazines, books, radio, television, and films.

Tom Paine is the latest of many biographies, which include such subjects as Frederick Douglass, Franklin, Washington, Jefferson, Jackson, Lincoln, Columbus, Thoreau, Mark Twain, Dorothea Lange, and Mary McLeod Bethune.

Among the many honors for his books are five nominations for the National Book Award as well as the Christopher, Jane Addams, Carter G. Woodson, Jefferson Cup, Washington Book Guild, Olive Branch, and Golden Kite awards. Many of his books have been chosen for the honor lists of the American Library Association, the National Council of Teachers of English, and the National Council for the Social Studies, as well as for the *New York Times* Best Books of the Year list.

Meltzer and his wife, Hildy, live in New York City. They have two daughters, Jane and Amy, and two grandsons, Benjamin and Zachary. Mr. Meltzer is a member of the Authors Guild, American PEN, and the Organization of American Historians.